What Others Are Saying

Unfortunately losing a child is not an uncommon event. Each mom or dad that has had that experience carries a heavy load of pain and sorrow. Sandy Lee knows that pain and sorrow. Only her pain doesn't subside! Her loss of a son in his mid 30's is filled with ongoing pain and sorrow... And mystery! Her son's remains have never completely been found. Sandy has opened her pain, her sorrow, and the mystery that consumes her as she takes the reader into the details of her son's death! If you enjoy mysteries, this book will hold your interest. You will marvel at the author's determination! You will question and wonder what really happened. And I hope you will join me in praying for the author's peace in the midst of her sorrow!

—Rick Larson
Author of 5:21

The bond between a mother and son is as strong in life as it is in death. Sandy Lee is relentless in the search for her missing son. She puts all of the pieces of the puzzle together, and still no arrests are made. She writes his fateful journey, and she clearly describes each hour, and each day as they drift into years. She screams inside to resolve this heinous crime.

A heartfelt story of a mother's anguish, fear and hope in the search to find out what has happened to her son. From the dark world of drugs and addiction to dealing with the Sheriff's Department, family and acquaintances, follow the search for the truth and the heartbreaking results she encounters.

To lose a child under any circumstances must be unbearable. To lose a child and not know why or how, and to have to search for that conclusion yourself is unthinkable.

I have known Sandy for about 10 years. I first met her on a San Francisco Mission trip that we took with a group from our local Church. She seemed to be a very compassionate person, and as I got to know her over the years I could tell she had a heart for the troubled, and for those people who sometimes, through no fault of their own, needed a helping hand in life. Whether it was fostering a young baby, or just providing a lunch for someone who was hungry, Sandy was there. Although I didn't know it at the time, Sandy had firsthand experience with a troubled son of her own, Darvie.

From deep within a mother's heart, Sandy tells the story of her personal search for her missing son. Despite the challenges, the continual frustrations, the 'dead ends', the heartaches, she sees God's hand everywhere. Never angry with God; never questioning him; but accepting that overall it is His hand at work. And just as she needed His strength in those early days when Darvie was first missing, she continually needs His strength as her seemingly fruitless search becomes never ending.

Sandy's faith and strength is an inspiration to anyone who has ever questioned the need for God or indeed his very existence. How can anyone who is going through what Sandy is going through accept that this is God's will? Read it to the end and you'll begin to understand the power of true faith. The power and strength that only someone who is hurting so much inside needs. Sandy's story would grip you if it was fictional. But her story is real and knowing that she is still living this nightmare will only make you wonder how she bears it at all. God is with her throughout, and she embraces His grace and presence. And miraculously, she seems to know that one day she will understand God's will. Maybe not in this world... but one day.

—Ron Patel
General Manager Black Oak Casino Resort
June 2014

No Unturned Stone: A Mother's Quest is a must-read for all mothers, counselors, and clergy. Sandy Lee has a way of telling her story that is both heartbreaking and authentic, as only a mother can. You can help others and yourself as you turn the pages to search for options to help Sandy work through the horror of searching for her son. I am sure there is someone in your family or neighborhood that you could help with the knowledge found in *No Unturned Stone: A Mother's Quest*. This book should be mandatory reading for anyone working in addiction recovery! This book is written to help others!

—Duke
Prison Chaplain, New Jersey

No Unturned Stone

Tracy,
all my
best to
you!

Sandy
Lee

No Unturned Stone

A Mother's Quest

SANDY LEE

"This story would grip you if it was fictional, but the story is real and knowing that this mother is still living the nightmare, will only make you wonder how she bears it at all."

TATE PUBLISHING
AND ENTERPRISES, LLC

Published by Tate Publishing & Enterprises, LLC
127 E. Trade Center Terrace | Mustang, Oklahoma 73064 USA
1.888.361.9473 | www.tatepublishing.com

Tate Publishing is committed to excellence in the publishing industry. The company reflects the philosophy established by the founders, based on Psalm 68:11,
"The Lord gave the word and great was the company of those who published it."

Book design copyright © 2014 by Tate Publishing, LLC. All rights reserved.
Cover design by Gian Philipp Rufin
Interior design by Mary Jean Archival
Author's picture—Courtesy of Steve Leontie Photography Twain Harte, California.

Published in the United States of America

ISBN: 978-1-63367-370-0
Biography & Autobiography / Personal Memoirs
14.10.17

Courtesy of The Union Democrat

"Radiance"—Rock Creek Wilderness, Oregon, courtesy of Marc Adamus

I dedicate this book to my son Darvis Beuford Lee Jr. whose life was so full of love and laughter. He could have continued to teach us all so many more things, if only he would have been given the time.

He loved me for who I was. Accepted me for who I wasn't.

While I was still in my teens, he changed my life. I have never been the same.

Acknowledgments

So many to thank...

If I would never have met my eighty-six-year-old friend Marge, this book probably would have never come to be. Her encouragement, her tears, and her belief in me kept me going. I will never forget the wonderful anticipation that I would have looking forward to the morning light when it was then that I would be able to read my next chapter to her.

You continued to encourage me on. Love you Marge.

My niece Lisa who helped me with the title for my book. When I said that I was thinking of "Unturned Stone," she said, "*No* Unturned Stone." She let me know that I was on a mother's quest, which totally explained the journey that I was already on.

Even before that moment, you gave me a reason for starting my story. Love your guts.

My longtime girlfriend Teresa, who was willing from the very beginning to read and keep on reading if it would have been necessary.

You gave me hope to continue. Loved you since second grade.

My friend Sharon who always loved that I read to her and shared my whole story before it was out. She encouraged me so much.

I enjoy being able to read out loud to someone, and you let me do that. Love you always. Thanks a million.

My daughter Kristie who is the smartest woman I know. She helped me with the editing of my book in a way that would never have been possible for me to do by myself. She taught me how to let my emotions out so that the reader could see inside my heart. I always knew what I felt, but I had forgotten that the reader did not. She taught me so much.

You drew close to me from the very beginning when this tragedy occurred. I could never have done this without you. I love you daughter of mine so very much.

My friend Peggy from high school, who got on board when I asked her to, and confirmed everything that my daughter had taught me.

Your words of encouragement kept me going. Love you girl.

Rick Larson who is a friend of mine that used to be my pastor. He willingly read whatever I asked him to. He encouraged me with his words. He confirmed what I already knew, that I had a story that needed to be told.

Thank you Rick. Much love.

I will forever be grateful for Gloria. One that I never knew before this all happened, but now love her as a friend. She made that first step forward that changed our lives. It was a direction that we needed to go. She took me wherever I wanted to go, to whomever I wanted to see. She truly would have done anything that I asked of her.

You are one of a kind. I will never forget you. I can't wait until you, Darvie, and I can get together. Love you so much.

Kerri…for loving that big brother of yours and supporting me so much with lots of love. As Darvie would say, "I love you, Carebear!"

Darvie's best friend Kathy who loved him from the beginning.

Thank you for giving him such a great friend. Pop's and I love you.

My husband Darvis who cried with me when he read some of the chapters that I asked him to read. He encouraged me every time. Although it is a story that breaks yours and my heart, you never asked me once not to write it. I am grateful for that. I love you honey.

To all our friends and family who actually helped us search for our son and those of you who have continued praying for us through the years, I will be forever grateful.

To those of you who were able to help us financially in the early days as we tried to do everything we could to find the answers. All the countless others who believed in me. You know who you are.

Your words gave me strength. They kept me motivated and determined to finish this book.

Thank you to all of you who loved Darvie and who saw beyond all his struggles and all his heartaches.

The love in my heart overflows for you all.

Last but not least, Marc Adamus, who so graciously allowed me to use his beautiful picture for the cover of my book. From the first time I ever saw it, I felt like the picture demonstrated, as the sunlight was shining through, just how God had overseen my journey and the many stones that were continually being turned.

You allowed the vision that I had from the very beginning, to use your picture for the cover of my book, to make everything come together so beautifully. Thank you so very much.

Preface

As the mother of a missing child and being a part of watching so many horrific things happen before my very own eyes, the words I found that continued to flow from my mouth were, "This is just so unbelievable! I have to write a book! Others need to hear this!"

The story I tell is my journey. Everything written is the way that I remember it to be and remember that I was told by the many people that I have encountered. I have tried to be as accurate as I can be to the best of my ability. My words are my opinion and mine alone. Any names other than my family are fictious. Names have been changed to protect the innocent. Any similarities to any event is only by accident.

Introduction

Gloria was watching out for a particular old tree for a landmark that would tell her that we were almost at the destination that we were searching for. Gloria said that the tree looked very creepy, and she felt that if only the tree could talk... the things that it would say.

We relied totally on her to get us to the right place. I just wanted to reach our destination as quickly as we could. I too felt like we did not have much time.

The darkness seemed to press in all around us as we finally arrived at an entrance to a dirt driveway. Hardly anyone would have been able to see it from the road. If you didn't know that it was there, you would most likely just pass it by.

After we all got out of our vehicles, Gloria, her husband, and friend said they were leaving. They said they would let us check out the property alone with the Tuolumne County Sheriff's Department.

Gloria said the place just gave her the *willies*.

We thanked them, and they went home.

Ever since Gloria told us what Mark had said about the landowner, all I kept thinking of was about this *crazy* landowner.

I also kept thinking that we needed to be careful and watch out for him. Every step we took, I kept expecting him to suddenly appear with a gun.

With flashlights in hand, we started down the driveway. We walked about one hundred feet, and then we came upon a big green iron gate.

On it in big red letters were painted the words:

"Keep the *F*—out." "You will hurt." "You will bleed."

What! You will *bleed*!?

Did I read that right?

You will bleed?

I was horrified!

I kept thinking, *Who writes such things?*

But what I could not understand was what I was seeing, was worse than even the words that I was reading.

Hanging down from the gate, tied together right in the middle of all the words, was our son's new work boots that he had just bought!

Prologue

I sometimes wonder...if the stories we heard at the very beginning will actually turn out to be the truth after all. Or at least, lead us to the truth?

I went looking the other day...going on another *tip*.

I will continue to check out all the leads that I ever get.

Today, I picked up Gloria, she is the one who has helped us out in so many ways. She took me to a house...me among strangers... living a life that I know not personally and got a woman there to tell us what she knows...what she has always known. She seemed to be speaking like she knew the truth. I guess many do, but it gave me a new hope. Something that I felt was different to go on. All the other leads have not led me to anything for quite awhile.

She speaks familiar names of people that I have felt have been responsible for our son's death. But she leaves out the extra names that we keep searching for...the other ones responsible.

She tells me she will dig deeper to find out more.

I get a big hug from the women there. Real hard, long, hugs. With us women, no matter what walks of life we come from; we love our children, and they try to understand my loss.

So we leave and drive once again out in the boonies. But this time, somewhere else. Somewhere that was unfamiliar to me. We were looking for the landmarks that the woman had given us. If we do not find them, she said she would come out with us when the weather is better.

I really don't care what kind of weather it is. I just want to find my son.

But I know it will be best to come back at a later time, when we are better prepared.

We go too far down the road, but that's okay. I just want to make sure. We make plans to come back soon to search for what we are looking for.

I always feel like, 'If I don't look, no one will'; or 'When I do nothing, nothing gets done'.

I do know that things are being done all the time though. God is working behind the scenes, in a way. One day when I leave this life, I will see how it all fit together making a beautiful tapestry.

My God doesn't need my help, but I know he uses me to help out. He has brought so many people in my path that I cannot deny his hand in it. He also knows, as long as I am able, I will not stop my investigating, until I find out the truth.

I have been told by some that I need to *relax* a little. Don't let this *consume* me. Maybe my own family members might beg to differ, but I really don't feel like this has consumed me more than it would any mother under these circumstances.

I am living in the town that I was born and raised in. I know so many people from so many walks of life around here. When someone says something to me, or I see an opportunity that I have been waiting for, I just act on it. I see God's hand in that all the time. I talk to whomever I see, that shows up in my path, that I have been looking for. I feel like so much is connected. That once I meet with someone and talk with them that they go to other people and start talking to them, and it starts connecting all the dots that will one day lead me to the truth.

I will leave no stone unturned.

It has been almost four years now since our thirty-six-year-old son, Darvis Lee Jr. went missing.

Four whole years!

How we have been able to endure all that we have had to endure, is beyond me. Unbelievable really…

I give God the glory for helping us to be able to endure it.

Four horrible long years! This is how it all began…

1

Our son Darvis, (whom I will call 'Darvie' from now on since it was his nickname, and because his dad, my husband, shared the same name), had been staying with us because he had just moved back to Sonora, California from Oregon. He and his wife had just recently split up.

He wanted to get a place of his own. He had just gotten accepted to continue his college classes online, and he was looking forward to starting a new life. In the past, he had wanted to be a physical therapist, but, more recently, he wasn't quite sure what kind of work he wanted to do, once he was done with his schooling.

He really wanted to have a son of his own one day, giving him his namesake.

So now with the new changes that were taking place in his life, I was thinking maybe he could begin to have the hope again, that his dream in the future may really come true.

Monday, October 18, 2010

Darvie had called me this morning, a little bit after 9:00 a.m., while I was uptown running errands with my mom. He left a message on my voice mail that I did not get to listen to at the time. In an uplifting voice, he said, "Hi, Mom! I was trying to get a hold of you to see if you got the mail and if my ATM card was in there. I'm looking at a couple of different places to rent, and I need to know...uh...how much money I have...so call me back or text me. Love you, bye!"

This exact message was what Darvie left on my voice mail. I was actually able to go back, record it, and put it on a CD. It is a message that I will cherish forever.

A short time later at 9:12 a.m., he texted me. "Did my ATM card come?"

I texted him back. "Yes."

At 10:54 a.m., he called again, and I was able to answer that call. He asked where his dad was, and I told him that he was at home.

That is the last time I have ever spoken to my son. Darvie then went to our house, and his dad helped him fill out a rental application. Darvis said that Darvie came to our house by himself and that he was in a good mood. Darvie told him that he thought that there was a good possibility that he was going to be able to rent the house. He wanted to drop off the rental application as soon as he could.

Darvis said that they talked mainly about the rental while he was at the house.

The house that he wanted to rent was in a town only a few miles from where we lived called Columbia.

Columbia is a California Gold Rush town located in the heart of the Mother Lode. When you walk down the main street of this town with all the sights, smells, and sounds, it is like you are walking back into time to a prosperous gold mining town, circa 1857. Merchants dressing in 1850's attire, a whiff of sarsaparilla coming from one of the local saloons, or horse hooves clopping bringing in the stagecoach are some of the things you may experience.

But just get to the outskirts of this charming town and danger can lurk at every corner. Sadly drugs are rampant in this community.

So Darvie picked up his ATM card at our house while he was there filling out the rental application. Darvis said that he stayed only about fifteen minutes but said that he would be back later that day, probably in a few hours.

My husband remembers that nothing seemed out of place. Darvie seemed to be acting totally normal in his behavior.

There was no warning given that this was the last time they would see each other.

But it was…

I remembered later on, that a few days earlier, after Darvie had opened up his checking and savings account, he had called me. He was telling me how much money he had. He was acting like someone was in his car with him, and I remember telling him that it wasn't a good idea for him to be talking out loud in his car about how much money he had. I didn't want whoever might be in the vehicle with him at the time to hear what he was saying. I never trusted any of his old acquaintances. I would never have wanted them to know his business.

We found out later that, on this day, Darvie did drop off the rental application with the landlord. And at 3:30 p.m., he had called the landlord to see if she had made her decision yet. He told her that he was really interested in renting the place, but she told him that she had not made her decision yet.

We believe this is the last phone call Darvie ever made.

Tuesday, October 19, 2010

At 1:45 p.m., the landlord, who had the rental house where Darvie had dropped off the application the day before, called Darvis. She had tried to call Darvie's phone, first, but had gotten no answer. She said that she had decided that she was going to rent the place to him. Darvis told her that we would try to get a hold of Darvie as soon as possible, and let him know. She said that she would hold the place for him until the following evening, but, if she did not hear back from him by then, she would have to rent it out to someone else.

Immediately I called him but got no answer. I then texted him, "Call Dad ASAP."

I knew wherever Darvie was, though, he may not get our messages right away. His cell service did not work well in our area, especially if he was in Columbia as I suspected.

I even got in my car and went to the only place I knew to go to look for him. It was to a house where a man named Kevin and his family lived that Darvie knew. I wanted to ask them if they had seen him.

The only reason that I knew Kevin and where he lived was because about two years earlier Darvie had fallen down a mine shaft. Kevin had been the one who had located Darvie way down in the mine so we could get a search team out to rescue him.

I will explain more about the mine incident in Chapter Three.

Kevin was not home at the time, but the people who happened to be there came outside to see me. It was a man that I did not know and Kevin's wife. They had acted like they had just seen Darvie recently, like maybe a couple of days earlier, but they did not give me any more information. As I was leaving, I noticed that their house and yard appeared to be like a junkyard would, with old abandoned vehicles spread out all over their yard, and garbage thrown everywhere.

This would be the first of many homes that I would see that were so neglected.

I did not know any of my son's current friends that were living up here. Darvie had been gone off and on for many years from this area. I did not know where to even go to look for him.

Several times, I tried calling him, trying to get a hold of him. I was so frustrated that he was not calling back since I knew he would be so happy when he heard that he got the rental house.

I saw that Darvie was getting such a good opportunity to start his life over.

To know, that he might miss that opportunity, made me sad, knowing how letdown he was going to be.

We found out, a couple of weeks later, after we received Darvie's cell phone bill that had come in the mail to our address that on this day at 10:01 a.m., a call was made from Darvie's cell phone to a home phone number of a woman named Debby. Debby was an ex-friend of our son.

Nothing good ever seemed to come from anyone being around Debby. She was a well-known drug dealer. A woman who had never had a child, it was only herself that she seemed to think of, and no one else. If she could bring someone down back into their addiction, she would have no problem with that. Just by looking at her, anyone could tell that the life she lived had done a major toll on her.

Time tracked on this call was one minute.

And immediately after that, another call was made from Darvie's cell phone to Debby's cell phone. Time tracked was also one minute.

These calls could have been a hang up each time the voice mail or answering machine came on; or they could have been a short message that was left on each; or it could have even been a quick conversation between two people saying something like, "It's done!"

Also, another number was called around 3:30 p.m. that day from Darvie's phone.

When the detective and my family tried to figure it out later on by looking at his cell phone records, it displayed a weird sequence of numbers.

We felt like it must have been his voice mail, being checked on his phone by someone. Perhaps the individual who now had his cell phone was checking to make sure that there was nothing on Darvie's voice mail that they did not want on there.

To think that someone had violated Darvie by taking his phone away from him and now had possession of it made me feel so helpless. I just didn't know what they had done to my son.

We believe Darvie did not make any of these calls mentioned above. We also believe at this point something had already happened to him.

His phone has never been found.

Wednesday, October 20, 2010

I went back to Kevin's house where I had been the day before. The same man who had been there before was hanging outside in the yard.

I asked him, "Is Kevin home?"

He said "Yes, but he is sleeping."

I then asked him, "Can you please go wake him up because I need to know if he has seen Darvie?"

The man then went in the house and found out that Kevin was not asleep but was actually eating. He invited me in.

The home was so dirty and cluttered with garbage inside. I would not have been able to find anything that would have been clean enough to sit on, if I had wanted to.

As soon as I got inside the house, I asked Kevin, "Have you seen Darvie?"

Kevin told me, "Darvie was over here on Sunday evening. He came over to our house real muddy."

Kevin seemed calm as can be as he ate and talked with me.

Kevin told me, "I had told Darvie, You better go in and take a shower because you can't go back to your folk's house looking like that!"

Kevin knew that we would wonder why he had gotten so muddy. Darvie would not have wanted to track dirt and mud all around our house. So it would only be normal for him to go to a friend's house like Kevin's and clean up.

Kevin said that Darvie had showered there but then had ended up spending the night.

Even now I still wonder why Darvie *really* showed up at Kevin's so muddy.

Kevin said that he had not seen Darvie since Monday morning.

He told me that Darvie might be over in Columbia at a woman's house named Anne.

He said Darvie had told him that he had been hanging around with Anne, the day he had gotten the rental application to fill out.

Kevin then gave me directions on how to get to an area around where Anne lived.

We found out later that Darvie had been at Kevin's house on Sunday evening, October 17, as Kevin had said.

Kevin's wife had actually taken a couple of pictures of Darvie in the early morning of October 18, a few hours before he had come over to our house to have his dad help him with the rental application.

Kevin's wife sent the two pictures to me via e-mail a few months after I had came over that day.

Seeing the pictures of Darvie, so soon before something was going to happen to him, was so very saddening to me.

I only wished that I could have forewarned him of the danger that was on its way.

I then went and drove to the area that Kevin had sent me to, so I could look for Anne. The area was on the outskirts of the main part of Columbia.

I stopped at the biggest house there to ask if they knew where Anne lived.

The house had the look of an old Victorian home. I knew from living in the area pretty much all my life, that it had at one time been very beautiful.

Now years later with looks of neglect, the old house appeared very weathered and seemed to be falling apart.

There was a woman in the house strangely watching me as I was walking closer to her house. I recognized her because I had attended the same high school as she had. I also knew that Darvie knew her because he had mentioned her to me years earlier. I asked her if she had seen Darvie. She said she had seen him, one day before. I told her that Darvie had gotten a place to rent, and that I was trying to find him so I could let him know.

She acted so strange in her behavior by not really saying much at all to me. She pointed up the hill to a small house when I asked her if she knew where Anne lived.

As I was walking up to the house where the woman said that Anne lived, I was relieved to know that at least I knew that Darvie was in the area.

I knocked on the door, but no one answered. It appeared that no one was home.

Being around these homes took me way out of my comfort zone. Although my house was far from perfect, these homes had a look about them that told a different story.

The people that hung around them; many coming off of drugs or still on drugs came from a different walk of life that I was used to. I didn't feel like I was better than them. I was just not as comfortable being around that environment because I did not really know where they were coming from. These were places that I had never been to before.

I remember all day wanting so bad for Darvie to call, because I knew by evening he would lose the rental.

At this point, neither I nor my husband was worried about him. We felt like there hadn't been any indication that anything had happened to Darvie. We just knew we hadn't heard from him and didn't know at all where exactly to look for him.

We had talked to our daughter Kristie and had let her know that we were having a hard time getting a hold of Darvie.

Thursday, October 21, 2010

My husband went to Anne's house again, and this time she was home. My husband talked with her and another man who was there to see if they had seen Darvie.

Darvis said that the name of Darvie's ex-friend Debby was brought up. Anne said that Darvie had been hanging around with her lately.

As soon as Darvis got home, told me what Anne had said, and I heard Debby's name, I was shocked!

I began to question why Darvie would be hanging around Debby because they were no longer friends.

Darvie had told me a few years back that he thought that Debby was into devil worshipping.

That really surprised me because I was firm in my faith in the Lord.

It was hard for me to think that anyone would dabble, let alone *want to* dabble in something that was the opposite of good. Darvie had said that Debby listened to chants of some kind, which he and I agreed did not seem normal.

He said that he had thought that she had tried to *poison* him one time with some corndogs that she had served him, but he couldn't prove it. I have also heard from a friend of Darvie's that one time Debby asked Darvie to get something out of a drawer for her, only for him to be encountered by a snake that had been put in there.

Darvie had told me that him and Debby had ended up having some disagreement in the past regarding some court case. He said she had wanted him to appear in court and lie for her which he did not want to do and never did.

For someone to tell me that Darvie had been hanging around Debby recently was unbelievable to me. He hadn't been back in town very long, and he was doing so well. Everyone who saw him knew how well he was doing.

What reason would ever make him go around *her* again?

It was later this same evening that Darvis and I decided that we were going to go the next morning to the bank to see if any activity had been used on his ATM card. After we were done doing that, we planned on going to look for him in the area where Debby lived.

Friday, October 22, 2010

My husband and I started out early in the morning, going right to the bank when it opened.

At first a woman at the bank said that they could not give us any information regarding Darvie's accounts. We mentioned to her that we had not heard from Darvie for a few days. We told her that we were getting very concerned because this was not normal behavior for him, and that we just needed to know if he had used his ATM card.

We had banked with them for many years and were well known by them.

All the women who worked at the bank even remembered who our son Darvie was that we were talking about. Even though he had only recently opened his checking and savings account, Darvie usually didn't appear anywhere without everyone remembering him when he left. He had that kind of personality. He never met a stranger.

The woman talked with some other women who were working with her at the bank. She then said that the only thing that she could tell us was that his ATM card had been used as of the evening before, on October 21 in our area.

Knowing that gave us some relief. But we also knew, when we found him that we would have all kinds of questions to ask him. It was all not making any sense to me.

We found out later when Darvie's bank statement came in the mail to our address, that his ATM card was used the evening before on October 21 at 10:22 p.m. for a purchase of $17.27.

By reading the bank statement, we could see that the purchase was made at a mini-mart. The charge had to be only to get gas because the mini-mart was already closed at that time of night.

When we checked with the mini-mart, we found out that there were no surveillance cameras outside. Ironically, my husband had known the previous owners, and he had been the one to put their surveillance cameras up inside the mini-mart, but that the previous owner had not had surveillance cameras put up outside. If only they would have!

Unfortunately, now we would never be able to see who used Darvie's ATM card.

We believe that his ATM was used as a credit card instead of as a debit.

If it would have been used as a debit, someone would have had to know the pin number.

We believe that Darvie was not the one who used his ATM card to get gas.

Next we went driving up to the area to try to find the house of his ex-friend Debby. The area was only a few miles off of the main road of Columbia, but it was a neighborhood that was out up in the hills. Looking around, the mountains are beautiful. Blackberry bushes are everywhere and greenery is all over the place. The roads wind around and around as you climb higher on the mountain. It appears very peaceful as you drive the road rarely ever meeting anyone else coming the opposite way.

The nights I am sure are filled with a lot more traffic for other reasons.

Unfortunately, these beautiful mountains house a whole bunch of rundown trailers that are sporadically spaced throughout one real big mountain.

There is raw garbage everywhere you look. Junk is thrown outside most of all the homes and over many of the embankments. Abandoned vehicles are left here and there with evidence of items taken off of them since the day that they had been abandoned. There are pit bulls roaming free at almost every home it seems.

The whole way as Darvis drove to that neighborhood, I kept looking over the embankments.

I started to worry that maybe Darvie had crashed his vehicle just like he had done only a year-and-a-half earlier around this same area.

I had so many unanswered questions that kept going through my mind.

We stopped at a couple of houses.

At one house we had to walk by all their piles of raw garbage and junk strewn around the yard, just so we could knock on someone's door and inquire if it was Debby's house. It was not.

My husband had been at Debby's home years earlier, when Darvie and Debby were still friends. Darvis had driven to pick up Darvie from Debby's place, but he couldn't remember where it was anymore.

Darvis was just about to turn around and go back down the road, but then I had a strong feeling that we needed to drive up the road some more.

As soon as we went up the road just a little ways, we spotted Darvie's car! It was in a driveway! The driveway of his ex-friend Debby!

I just couldn't wait to see him! We were so relieved because we had finally found him!

We hurriedly drove into the driveway and parked right in front of Darvie's car that was backed up in the driveway. We got out and started walking quickly up the walkway until we noticed all the garbage cluttered around. We had only a few feet in between the walls of raw garbage and stench, as we made our way up the driveway.

I was alarmed as we began to notice all the animal bones that were displayed out in her yard like decaying trophies. There were newspapers stacked all around. Big rocks covered the ground. Tarps covered miscellaneous items. There was a mess everywhere we looked.

We still couldn't wait to see Darvie! We had so much to say to him!

But it appeared that no one was anywhere in sight.

Where was our son?

2

Friday, October 22, 2010—Continued

We quickly continued up the dirt driveway toward Debby's house.

A man suddenly stepped out of a toolshed, and we asked him, "Is Darvie here?"

Of course we assumed that he was.

The man was unfamiliar to us. He shook my husband's hand and introduced himself as "Mike".

We found out later that Mike was a fake name that he was using.

"Mike" said, "No, he left a couple of days earlier with some people. I've been wondering when he was coming back because his car has kind of been in our way in the driveway."

Darvis said, "We can have the car towed if you want us to?"

"Mike" said, "No, that's okay."

Right away I thought that was weird that he mentioned that the car was in their way, but yet he did not want the car to be towed away.

"Mike" seemed all calm and collected.

Even though the place was a mess, "Mike" had mentioned that he and Darvie had cleaned up Debby's yard.

Then "Mike" told me, "Darvie and I have been friends for about ten years, and Debby and Darvie are good friends too."

That was when I looked him straight in the eye and said as certain as I could, "No, Darvie is not friends with her."

I was beginning to feel disgusted with all the things he started to say.

"Mike" told me that he had dated my son's estranged wife years ago. I wondered at the time why he would be telling me that. Why would I care?

For no reason really, Darvis mentioned to "Mike" that Darvie's ATM card had been used.

Darvis and I were not thinking that anyone had hurt Darvie or had done anything to him at this point. We were just trying to think aloud and try to figure some things out.

We believe now that "Mike" had taken possession of Darvie's ATM card somehow. We believe that "Mike" was the person that had also used Darvie's ATM card the night before on October 21. We also believe that "Mike" used the card to fill up some gas cans that we found almost a week later on some property that was linked to Darvie. After "Mike" was told that Darvie's ATM card had been used, we believe that the ATM card was probably destroyed right away after that.

"Mike" told Darvis that he would always have Darvie's back.

This statement has sickened us every time we have heard those words spoken by anyone since.

Darvis gave "Mike" one of his business cards that had our phone number on it so that "if and when" Darvie showed back up there again "Mike" would let us know.

I was discouraged that Darvie was not there. I kept wondering if he really was in the house. I do not know what even gave me that feeling. I did not like the way things were going down.

To me nothing was matching up, so I asked "Mike", "Are you sure he isn't in the house?"

He said, "No, he's not."

I felt that "Mike" was very untrustworthy. I had a gut feeling that something just was not right.

When I expressed my feelings to Darvis as we got in our vehicle, he too agreed that he was feeling the same uneasiness as I was. We felt if Darvie was not safe, we needed to tow his car out of there. It was like we wanted to get anything that belonged to Darvie as far away from these people and as quickly as we could.

I remember as we were driving away past the house I looked up and saw "Mike" coming out of the house. For some reason, I questioned Darvis of why he thought "Mike" was coming out of the house.

Darvis said, "Oh, he probably went inside for a moment to put up the business card I gave him."

I had a split second thought of, *What if Darvie was in there being held against his will? What if he was unconscious? What if "Mike" went in to make sure that Darvie was exactly where he had left him?*

But as quickly as that horrible thought came to me, it went away and I figured Darvis was probably right. Then I began to just wonder where Darvie really was.

We then went to a local towing company nearby. We were familiar with the towing company. We got a tow truck right away to follow us up to where Darvie's car was parked. We let them know at the towing yard that we did not have a key to the vehicle. They knew that they would have to use a Slim-Jim if all the doors ended up being locked.

Darvie's car was parked backwards in the dirt driveway. So when we got back to the car and checked it out, we noticed that all the doors were locked except for the driver's side. Darvis and I assumed that Darvie had his car keys since "Mike" had acted like he had not been able to move the car.

The driver's side was very close to the side of a bank. The tow truck driver had a hard time getting in the car because of how close to the bank it was. The car was not really blocking the driveway though. There was room on the other side of the car in the driveway where obviously Debby parked her vehicle when she was home.

Darvie's car was a four-door and the condition of it inside and out seemed okay.

I didn't even want to tell "Mike" that we were taking the car, but Darvis asked me if I had told "Mike" that we were towing it out of there. Darvis acted like he wanted me to go tell him so I went up to the house and knocked on the door. When "Mike" answered the door right away, I told him that we were towing the car away.

I didn't care at the time if "Mike" liked what we were doing or not. I felt like we were controlling the situation now.

I again asked "Mike" as he walked down the driveway with me what I had asked him earlier. Looking toward the house I asked him, "Are you sure Darvie's not in there?"

"Mike" replied, "Yeah. Why would I lie to you?"

I said, "Because I think it's weird that you don't know who he left with."

After a pause, "Mike" replied, "We weren't here when he left".

I then asked him for Debby's phone number.

Again he paused and said, "I don't call our number so I don't know it".

Was this guy just lying through his teeth to us? Had he done something to my son?

I wasn't concerned enough at this point, to *really* think those things could be true. It just seemed like my mind was playing all kinds of tricks on me. It seemed like I would be overreacting at that point if I called the Sheriff's Department.

Looking back now though I wish we would have waited right there and made that call. I don't know if it would have made a difference, but it may have allowed us to find things of interest in Debby's home.

Darvis and I wondered if "Mike" had done something to Darvie and then taken his car since he was not giving us straight answers. Maybe "Mike" thought that no one would be coming around looking for the car so he just started using it.

We have since been told from people in Debby's neighborhood that Darvie's car had been moved around in Debby's driveway. They told us that the car had been facing forward as well as backward. This all happened during the few days Darvie's car was left at Debby's and Darvie was not around.

For me to think that "Mike" might have hurt my son and then nonchalantly drove his car around sickens me. Just thinking about how calm "Mike" was when we arrived the first time at Debby's house sickens me worse. And to think if he was guilty of doing something to Darvie a few days earlier and could act "normal" just like that was almost too much for me to believe.

Whether any of this is true or not, we may never know.

Do I now think that "Mike" had access to Darvie's car keys *before* we came by that day and found Darvie's car? Absolutely!

One thing that we were sure of, the more we thought of it was that Darvie would not have left his vehicle and went with someone else. Darvie had a reliable car that he could drive anywhere. Leaving with someone and driving around would not have been something he would have wanted to do. Darvie liked to be in control. Having his own car was something that he took pride in.

We then had his car towed to our house. My husband had it put back close to our garage, and he put another vehicle close to it in the front. That way when Darvie came to pick it up, if we were not at home, he would have to wait for us so we could talk to him. We knew Darvie would come in our house "if and when" he came to get his car. However none of what was happening was normal. We wanted to make sure no one came if we were gone and try to take his vehicle.

We did not want to take any chances.

We also knew that if Darvie had been getting our text messages or calls he would have called us by now. He had always kept in contact with us. There were never more than a couple of days at the most that would ever go by that we did not hear from him, no matter where he was.

Again I began to get a sick feeling down deep inside. Where was our son!? What had someone done to him!?

Later this same day, Darvis and I went back to Debby's house and found her home. She came out on her small front deck, and we asked her if she had seen Darvie. She said she had not seen him recently. She gave us her cell and her home phone number when I asked for it.

I quickly wrote down the numbers.

My husband was the one who mainly talked with her. I did not trust her at all. She acted calm and even tried to show a little concern. I just knew Darvie and Debby had not been friends for quite awhile and Darvie had never trusted her completely.

As we walked back down the driveway to leave, I noticed on Debby's dashboard in her vehicle an animal skull. With disgust I walked away.

Saturday, October 23, 2010

All weekend long I struggled with the thought of should I call the local sheriff's office to make a Missing Person's Report or not. I didn't want to do anything extreme and make a big deal about something that I had no reason to make a big deal about.

Even though Darvie was not surfacing, I still held on to the hope that soon we would get a call from him. My husband left me in charge of when to make the call. I talked with Kristie, and some other family members and friends about our concerns.

As I was encouraged by family and friends to make the call, I kept having a hesitation to finally do it.

I think that I knew that once I finally did make the call; I would have to realize that something probably was terribly wrong.

I just wanted Darvie to show up and make everything better.

Kevin, that friend of Darvie's that I had visited at the beginning of all this, called me up. He wanted to see if we had gotten a hold of Darvie yet.

As we began to talk and I mentioned Debby and "Mike" it was then that he told me that "Mike's" name was really Mark and that Mark was Debby's boyfriend.

It was then that I realized that the guy had given us a fake name.

Kevin said that Darvie and Mark had gotten in an argument a few days earlier, and Darvie had to jump out of a window to get away and that is why he came over to Kevin's house so muddy.

I hardly knew this guy Kevin so I did not know if I could believe the things that he was telling me.

He seemed to care about what might have happened to Darvie though.

Now with me knowing that Mark had given us a fake name, it made me start to realize that something terrible must be up.

As I suspected, Mark and Debby were definitely people that could not be trusted.

I called Darvis right away and gave him this new information.

Later on when questioned by the sheriff's office, Kevin changed part of his story. He said that the situation that involved Mark and Darvie getting in an argument and Darvie having to jump out of a window had happened a long time ago.

We believe if this incident had ever really happened, then it would have had to have been more recent, just as Kevin had originally told me. We believe this because Mark had previously been in prison for quite awhile and had just recently been released. We also found muddy clothing in the trunk of Darvie's car.

This was just the beginning of people starting to tell us all kinds of stories. We could never get a straight answer out of any of them. We never knew if what was said was truth or if it was a lie.

However I have always figured that there was some truth in every lie.

Sunday, October 24, 2010

I called Kristie and asked her to call around to other relatives in Modesto, California where Darvie used to frequent at times through the years. I wanted her to see if any of them had seen or heard from him.

She made the calls but told me that no one had seen or heard from him recently.

On this evening I finally made the call to the Tuolumne County Sheriff's Department to make a Missing Person's Report.

I had pretty much been praying about it and gave myself until Sunday evening to make the call if I had not heard from Darvie.

I knew the time had come.

I also knew that it would probably be something that would be put in our local paper so doing this, being extreme or not, it was now going to happen.

I made the call. It was now a done deal.

We all began to worry.

Kristie and our son-in-law Bobby both made plans to take off work the next day and come up to help us look for Darvie. They lived almost two hours away so they would have to leave early in the morning to head up.

I think we all began to feel it in our hearts that something very bad had happened to Darvie.

Monday, October 25, 2010

My husband had contacted Detective Bob at the Tuolumne County Sheriff's Department who he had known for many years.

Detective Bob had known Darvie in the past, and Darvis asked him to please take on the case. He said that he would. We trusted him and knew that he would do the best job that he could in helping us to find our son.

Kristie and Bobby came up with our two granddaughters. Our granddaughters were going to stay at home with our younger son for the day.

We decided to get missing person flyers made.

We wanted to go around to four different towns nearby. Columbia, Sonora, Jamestown, and Tuolumne City. We wanted to put the flyers up anywhere we could find a place.

We went as soon as the local office supply business opened and we waited for the copies to be made.

We had about one hundred copies of the missing person flyers printed out.

We began to tell people that we encountered about our concerns. They in turn began showing their concern also.

My heart was heavy as we began driving through the towns. It was all so unbelievable.

When we got to each town, Bobby would get out with stapler in hand and begin putting a flyer up at every advertising board and place that looked like people in town would see it.

As we continued to see people in town that we knew, we began to mention to them that Darvie was missing.

We were on a mission now and nothing it seemed could stop us.

We even went back to the area where we had found Darvie's car and started knocking on people's doors.

We began putting the flyers up in as many different locations in that neighborhood that we could find. We were willing to do anything.

A local water company was installing fire hydrants in the whole neighborhood at the time, and all the gravel roads were now getting paved. Road work was being done constantly as we tried to make our way through it all, to put up our flyers.

Most everyone we talked with in the neighborhood acted like they knew nothing.

As we walked around that area handing a flyer out to every vehicle that passed by, I had an uneasy feeling.

It was like I knew that there were people in that area that knew *exactly* where Darvie was, but they were not saying a word.

My son was missing! Please Lord, help us find him!

Tuesday, October 26, 2010

Kristie and Bobby came back up again. The four of us spent the day passing out more of the missing person flyers. We knew that we had to work fast to let as many people as we could know, so that maybe someone would be able to help us.

As much as we were getting the word out, the discouragement inside our hearts could be felt by all of us.

Just as I had expected, the notice regarding the Missing Person's Report that I had made had been published in our local newspaper. Friends and acquaintances began to contact us offering any assistance that they could.

Toward evening Kristie and Bobby headed back home. They both had important jobs that they were needed at back in their town where they lived. Seeing them give all they had to try to find Darvie too, just broke my heart.

Awhile later there was a knock on our front door.

Two women and a man whom we did not know were standing there when I opened the door. They told me that they were friends of Darvie's, and that they thought they might know where he was.

My heart leaped in my chest!

I thought that "finally" we were going to find out where he was! I quickly let them in.

One of the women introduced herself as Gloria, and she did most of the talking.

She told us that she knew Debby and Mark, and that Mark had told her *a story* only a few days before we had picked up Darvie's car.

Gloria said that on Tuesday October 19, she had stopped over at Debby's house thinking that Darvie was there because she had seen his car parked in the driveway. She said Darvie's car had been parked in the driveway facing Debby's house.

A friend of Gloria's told her, that later that same day when she stopped by Debby's house, Darvie's car was backed in the driveway, facing the road. The same way we had found it.

When Gloria arrived at Debby's house, Debby's vehicle wasn't there, so she knew Debby wasn't home. She figured that obviously Darvie wasn't there either, because Debby had a video camera running all the time inside her house, and anyone, who was in the house, could see what was going on in the driveway.

She knew Darvie would have come out if he had been there. Gloria said that she had not even gotten out of her car, and she was just about to get out and leave a note, when Mark suddenly scared her as he showed up quickly from behind at her passenger window. She said that Mark told her Debby was working, and, when she asked him where Darvie was, it suddenly dawned on her and she looked at Mark and said, "Debby had Darvie go work with her, didn't she?"

Gloria said that was when Mark looked at her very strange and said, "If you promise not to say anything to anyone, I'll tell you what happened."

Mark told Gloria that earlier he and Darvie had taken Mark's truck and they had drove way out on some property, about five miles away.

Gloria was familiar with the location Mark was talking about because it was the same place that Mark and Debby had actually taken Gloria before, to look in some abandoned mines.

Previously Gloria had an experience with Mark and Debby that she never wanted to repeat. Mark had taken Gloria way back inside one of the abandoned mines while Debby remained outside by the entrance. Mark's behavior, Gloria said, was very strange because he was acting like there were other people around them, and so after awhile, she finally found her way back out of the mine, and as soon as Debby saw her come out, Debby said, "Oh, I was thinking he had done something to you!"

Gloria wondered, what kind of a friend was Debby to think such a thing and not come in to possibly help, and again, why would Debby be with someone like Mark if she thought he might do something to her. Gloria said that she wanted to get out of there as quickly as she could and never go back.

Mark told her, "Darvie and I were just hanging out on the property. I was trying to take a part off of a rock crusher, and Darvie was down below just messing around cutting brush. All of a sudden we heard a vehicle coming with their music real loud."

"But then, it was completely quiet. We heard someone get out of their vehicle. I told Darvie to go hide, and I went and hid under a boat. Darvie just wouldn't be quiet and he kept moving around in the brush. And then I saw the landowner walk by carrying a Mossberg gun. It was within inches from me."

"We stayed hidden until the landowner left and drove away. Then we headed back to my truck. I had Darvie walk about thirty feet behind me at all times, and I was walking ahead. Darvie kept fiddling around with his phone, and I kept telling him to knock it off. I finally made it up to the road. When I turned around, Darvie was gone."

Gloria then said to Mark, "And you left and didn't go back to look for him? Why would you just leave him there?"

She said Mark said, "I drove back and forth on the road for awhile and revved up my motor but then when he didn't come, I finally left."

Gloria said that Mark told her that he was planning on going back out there again.

It worries me to think Mark could have gone back and what he may have done while he was out there again.

She said he then made some derogatory remarks about Darvie.

Even after Gloria had been told this story by Mark, she said she still did not think anything had happened to Darvie. She knew that Darvie would find his way back regardless if he had been left out there.

On Saturday October 23, she had stopped again back at Debby's house. Darvie's car was gone from the driveway, so thinking that Darvie had finally come back and taken his car like she knew he would, Gloria felt a lot better.

Once inside the house, Gloria mentioned to Debby how relieved she was that Darvie had obviously made it safely out of that property, since his car was gone. Then Debby told Gloria that Darvie didn't pick his car up at all, that his parents came and had it towed away.

Gloria had thought that Mark wasn't even at home, so she started telling Debby what Mark had previously told her. She said Debby acted like she didn't even know Mark had told Gloria anything at all. Even at that, Gloria said that Debby still acted like she didn't care where Darvie was. Debby told Gloria that Mark could tell her all about it when he woke up from his nap

Gloria realized then that Mark *was* there.

She said it wasn't long after Debby said that to her when Mark finally came walking out of the bedroom.

Mark told Gloria that my husband had mentioned that Darvie's ATM card had been used the previous night.

She said, "Oh that's good because Darvie would have had to be the one using it since you would have to know the pin number."

Gloria said it was then that Mark strangely looked straight at her and said, "Not if you use it as credit."

Gloria thought that Mark was acting very weird about it all.

It was only when Gloria saw one of our flyers at a neighbor's house a few days later that she realized that Darvie was actually "*missing*"!

And she knew the person who had admitted to being with Darvie last.

At this point Gloria said that she took off in a vehicle to find Mark and Debby. When she saw them driving toward her, she said they just drove right by. So she went around another way and met up with them quickly as they must have drove very fast to get to Debby's house, but then Gloria blocked them with her vehicle. She then jumped out of her vehicle and confronted both Mark and Debby.

She said, "This is a bunch of bull. I'll give you an hour and a half, and if you do not go and tell his parents where he was last seen, I will!"

With that Gloria took off.

Gloria and Debby had been best friends for about ten years, she told us.

They have never been friends since.

Gloria was very caring toward us and seemed to really care about Darvie. She appeared worried as she talked with us like we may not have much time.

With concern in her voice Gloria began telling us where the location was where Mark had said him and Darvie were last together.

Even though Darvis and I had lived in this area for years, neither one of us were familiar with that particular area.

I asked her, "Can I call the sheriff's office and get a hold of the detective? Then would you take us all out to the area?"

Gloria, her husband and friend, all agreed that they would.

Darvis called and got Detective Bob on the phone. He agreed to meet us at a certain spot in the nearby town of Columbia.

We quickly called Kristie and told her all that had happened.

She said they had just finally gotten home.

But they made plans to come back up again, and we knew that we would see them when we got back home that night.

I could not wait to go!

Now all I was thinking about was that eight days had already passed.

We just had to get there soon so we could find him!

Although our son was a survivor, being out that long without food or water, I just did not know how much longer he could last.

All I hoped was that my son would hold on until we were able to get to him.

3

My son, Darvie, was one of those kinds of people that when you met him, you instantly connected. You liked what you saw. He was always fun loving and made you laugh just by being with him.

Thinking of how it all began makes my heart happy.

A little boy with the brightest blond hair, falling down kind of long over his big brown eyes, was one that won my heart over, right from the very start. His little chubby cheeks and tummy that stuck out over his shorts was an adorable sight to see. He had a whole lot of love in him from the time he was very little. His funny personality even from such an early age kept him full of giggles. At times, he would slobber as he laughed if he got laughing too hard. Of course, it would make everyone start cracking up laughing just at the sight of that. I think it truly was love at first sight for him and me.

Darvie was born in Modesto, California and grew up mainly with his sister, our daughter Kristie. She was only two and a half years older than him. They were the kind of siblings that were best friends. They spent hours together playing in each other's rooms. Whatever his older sister would want to do, Darvie was right there wanting to do it too. If they got in an argument it wasn't long before the giggles would come, and it would be as if nothing had happened between them.

He was a very caring little boy as was evident in all the crayon drawings that I received on almost a daily basis, letting me know how much love there was in his little heart. He liked to curl up in my arms and, boy, did I love kissing his soft little forehead each night as I tucked him into bed! One of my fondest memories will always be winding up his favorite teddy bear and as it played music I would walk out of his room like a wound up toy. He always seemed to like that and he would giggle.

As he grew up I had made a Fred and Barney pillow for him and even in his preteens I captured a picture of him sleeping with the pillow beside him.

I tried to take my kids most of the time to church as they were growing up. We mainly lived in Modesto and Ceres, California, until Darvie was almost ten years old, and then we moved to my hometown of Sonora, California. So whether it was in Modesto, Ceres, or Sonora that we went to church, my children learned early about the Lord and they memorized scripture at times.

The twenty-third Psalm was always Darvie's favorite. That verse had been a comfort to him for when he often found himself down and out in the years to come, he would tell me that he would recite it over and over again.

> The Lord is my shepherd; I shall not want. He maketh me to lie down in green pastures: He leadeth me beside the still waters. He restoreth my soul: He leadeth me in the paths of righteousness for His name's sake. Yea, though I walk through the valley of the shadow of death, I will fear no evil: for thou art with me; thy rod and thy staff they comfort me. Thou preparest a table before me in the presence of mine enemies: thou anointest my head with oil; my cup runneth over. Surely goodness and mercy shall

follow me all the days of my life: and I will dwell in the
house of the Lord forever.

By early 1984, after nine different moves and five different
schools, we had moved our family permanently back to Sonora.
Our kids would move with us five more times and go to three
more schools, two different than before.

And ever since we came back up here, Darvis and I have never
left this area.

Sonora is in the beautiful Sierra Nevada foothills. The town
still holds onto its historic charm with many of its buildings
dating back to the 1800s. Gold mining was the driving force back
in the 1850s. Sonora is considered California's Mother Lode.

There are mountains everywhere you look, and anyone coming
from the valley below up to our area is able to see to the west,
a table mountain formation caused by volcanic eruptions many
years ago.

Breathtaking views of snow peaked mountains are always in
the far distance in the winter for all to see.

Only a fifteen minute drive in the spring, summer, or fall can
take you up to the wonderful smell of pine where sixty feet pine
trees make their home. It is like being in a forest with tall trees
everywhere. Usually that is only how far you need to go to find
snow in the winter when our town of Sonora doesn't have any.

Going down only a few miles from Sonora is a town called
Jamestown. It was known for its underground quartz mines back
in the late 1800s. In 1898, a steam railroad was built to connect
our foothills to the valley below. Jamestown was the headquarters
to the railroad. A lumber mill not far away in Tuolumne City
provided the logs for the railroad to transport. Railroads were
built far into the woods to branch lines where other lumber
mills were.

So if it's Sonora, Columbia, Jamestown, or Tuolumne City, it
is still basically the same community only a few miles away from

each other. As beautiful and historic as these towns are, again, you don't have to go far, and drugs are readily available if needed. It's almost like it is an epidemic here.

Well when Darvie was still young, drug abuse had already started in our community.

Darvie liked to play outdoors like all the other kids did.

If it wasn't with his cousins Larry and Kirt that he was hanging around with that lived across the street, it would have been with a friend or two that lived nearby.

But unfortunately in 1986 while we were living in the town of Jamestown, something happened to Darvie when he was not quite twelve years old. Something that would change his life forever.

On this particular day, he was out by himself riding his bike in the neighborhood that we lived in. It was a subdivision where all the houses were right next to each other with each having a fenced backyard.

Earlier I had seen him on his bike near the entrance of our neighborhood when I was arriving home in my car. I had stopped and talked to him for a moment. When I was about to drive away to go to our house which was just at the end of the road, I told him to be home before dark.

A while later around 5:00 p.m., I had heard him come back, and he was in the garage. Darvie had brought his bike home but went out to play again. I had questioned at the time to myself where he had went. I figured he was just going out again in the neighborhood since it was still early spring and still light outside. I knew that he would be back before it got dark as I had told him to.

It wasn't until the sun was beginning to go down that I started really wondering where he was. I knew that he would have always come home before it was dark. He knew I would be fixing dinner and that soon it would be time for him to come eat. Besides he was just a young boy, and he would have wanted to be home with us at this time.

My daughter Kristie and I ran out to our front yard and began calling for him as we stood in our yard. Within a few minutes when we realized he wasn't coming, Kristie and I got in our car, and I started driving around our neighborhood looking for him. I even drove outside our subdivision passing by a pond nearby, quickly checking to see if he was there. We continued to call out for him. I remember really feeling scared because something like this had not ever happened before. It was not like Darvie to not be home by now.

When we got back to the house and found out that Darvie still wasn't there, I called Darvis frantically. Then I called the Tuolumne County Sheriff's Department.

By the time my husband came home we just knew something had happened to Darvie. I remember my husband kicking our porch post trying to let out some of his frustration. None of us knew what to do as we waited for law enforcement to arrive.

I was so happy when an officer showed up shortly after that and Darvis and I began to tell him what was going on.

We also told him that a couple of weeks earlier Darvie had been walking after school, taking the railroad tracks home. The tracks were near the school, and it was a shorter way to get home. Many kids walked that way.

Darvie had said that a man came out of nowhere and had suddenly grabbed him.

Though Darvie was still not a very big boy yet, he said that when the man grabbed him, somehow they had both fell down. It was then that Darvie was able to quickly get up and run away.

I think the knowledge of knowing someone had tried to kidnap him only a couple of weeks earlier, and now we didn't know where he was, brought on even more anxiety for us.

We had called the Tuolumne County Sheriff's Department at the time the previous incident had happened, but we still did not know who had tried to kidnap him and to this day we still don't know.

The waiting was unbearable! It wasn't until over two long hours later from the time we began searching for Darvie that the officer that we were talking to received the long awaited call.

We were standing outside in front of our home when we heard the news. Darvie had just been found a few miles away from our home!

He was okay!

My heart was so relieved!

Our little boy was going to be all right!

The officer that was with us said that he was told by another officer who had responded to the call, that Darvie had ended up at a house where he had frantically banged on the door. When the people opened the door and saw this young boy just standing at their front door looking very frightened, they quickly called the Tuolumne County Sheriff's Office.

Darvie was now being picked up by that officer and would soon be on his way home to us.

I couldn't wait to see him! Darvis, Kristie, and I were so happy! I was so thankful to the Lord that he had been found.

At the beginning, I don't think any of us thought anything bad had happened to him.

I just figured Darvie had ended up somewhere and then it had just gotten dark. Maybe then he had become too frightened to find his way home. It was not in his character to roam very far away from home. At the time, I did not realize that Darvie had actually been found too far for him to have wandered out alone by himself.

As the other deputy's car came into sight, our emotions could hold back no longer. When Darvie got out of the vehicle, we just couldn't hug him enough. Just holding him and knowing he was okay made my heart so very happy.

Being so relieved to have him back home with us, we had not noticed at first the condition that he arrived back in.

Then we noticed…

With horror we realized that one of his shoes were gone. Also missing was his favorite wristwatch, which Darvie had not even noticed was gone, until I noticed and brought it up to him. His T-shirt was torn at the top in the middle, down a ways.

We noticed there was some kind of white substance on his pants which we thought was "lime".

We later had been told that Darvie had been found not too far from a limekiln that we had in our area.

Darvie was obviously shaken up. The officer that had been helping us, questioned him in his patrol car.

I think we were all just in shock.

But then after Darvie was home he began to tell us the horrible details of what had happened. He told us how he had arrived where the officer had found him.

He said that after he had brought back his bike to the house that evening, he was walking down the street in our neighborhood.

He was just around the corner from our house, when a truck pulled up beside him with three guys in it. He said that the passenger door was suddenly opened, and he was grabbed and pulled inside the vehicle where he was held below the dashboard.

After a couple of hours, the three men ended up dropping him off all alone on a road. Then they quickly drove away and left him there.

Darvie said the whole time he was with the three men all he kept thinking about was a little boy named Adam who had also been taken away not quite five years earlier, the day after Darvie's seventh birthday. That little boy had been killed and Darvie was so afraid that something like that might happen to him too.

As soon as he was let out of the truck, he said he ran as fast as he could. He said he ran to the first house he found which wasn't too far away. He then banged on the door and when a man answered, Darvie told him that someone had kidnapped him and dropped him off nearby. The people in the house immediately called the police.

Darvie never had a hard time talking with me so I wasn't surprised when the next evening, late at night he started telling me a little about what had went on while he was gone with those three guys.

He said while he was under the dashboard of their truck, he kept being told by them to not look at them, but he noticed that the man sitting in the middle was wearing a ski mask the whole time.

He said that the middle man had many of his teeth missing which I could tell had frightened him.

The horrible image of that particular middle man, would stay with him for many years later.

Darvie said that they had even stopped at someone's house, and he had been kept in a bedroom for awhile.

He told me that they were doing weird sexual stuff around him.

Even though Darvie had started to share these things with me, I never really found out *exactly* what went on.

I don't know if I just didn't ask the right questions because maybe I was just too afraid to find out.

I was horrified to think that men would take my innocent little boy minding his own business, out of his own secure neighborhood and do unheard things to him.

What they had done to him would eventually mess his life up tremendously.

I wanted those men found!

As Darvie began sharing these things with me, I then told Darvis and then we called the Tuolumne County Sheriff's Department again and the same officer came right out and talked with Darvie awhile.

I had washed all of Darvie's clothes the day before so I had made it impossible for any evidence to be checked out.

A few days later I had to take Darvie to the sheriff's department. They said that they wanted to talk to him. When we arrived, a deputy told me that they wanted to talk to Darvie by himself.

At the time I did not realize that I could have refused to allow him to go in by himself. If I would have known that of course I would never have allowed it.

Looking back now I sure wish I would have insisted on being with him while he was being questioned.

It wasn't until we left the sheriff's office, and we were driving away that Darvie began to cry. He told me how the officers did not believe the things that he had told them.

He said that they told him, "Your story isn't adding up. We think that you are lying. You need to just come out and tell us the truth of what *really* happened."

When I heard that, I was so angry and I couldn't wait to get home so that I could call my husband at his work and tell him. Darvis contacted the sheriff's office to confront them on it.

I realized that the tactics that they used were for them to try to make sure if someone was telling the truth or not. But to do that to a young innocent boy of only eleven years old was not the way to go about it in my opinion.

However nothing further was ever even done on this case.

Our family had no idea who had picked Darvie up that night. We knew there was no way we would ever find out unless someone came forward. Darvie did not know who they were either. My heart was broken for him.

Even years later, there was confusion of what had really happened that evening but I knew that Darvis and I were the adults back then, and our son had only been a child, and we knew something terrible had happened to him.

All that transpired with those three men, changed everything.

For some reason back then in 1986, we never asked a bunch of questions. It was kind of like, 'If you don't talk about it, it never happened'.

The story saying that our son had been kidnapped was put in our local newspaper though.

Kids at school began to make fun of Darvie and give him a hard time. Kids really can be so cruel. I felt so sorry for my son.

Shortly after this all happened, we moved back to Sonora and bought our first home and our children switched schools once again.

This is the time where Darvie met a girl by the name of Kathy who would become a friend that he would consider the best of them all.

They talked for hours on the phone and as Kathy recalls, he was the only one who had the first cool cordless phone. He would walk all around our house talking to her while she said that she was stuck on a phone that possibly had the longest cord attached that she would try to stretch even farther to be able to talk in secret with her best friend.

Many of times I would hear Darvie and her crack up about the things that they were talking about. Kathy's mother always allowed Kathy to talk to Darvie even if she was grounded which happened so often that even I would begin to ask Darvie, "What did she get grounded for *now?*"

When Kathy was not allowed to talk to any of her friends, her mom always made an exception with Darvie. Their special relationship continued for the rest of his life.

Wanting Darvie to get some help from what had happened to him while he was kidnapped, I contacted the Victim Witness Program. They offered their services, and so we did have Darvie go to some counselors at the beginning right after it happened. Darvie never felt comfortable with the counselors that he was going to, especially the first one we took him to, seeing as it was an old man.

I wanted to do right by him but I never knew what the right thing to do really was.

Six years later when Darvie got close to turning eighteen years old, we sold our home, bought some property, and moved back to Jamestown again. Darvie would go to counseling sometimes even then, but would quit shortly after his first visit. Then if he started going again, many times he never went back to the same person. Each counselor would want him to tell them about what happened, and he never wanted to keep rehashing it over and over again. So he made many excuses to me about why he didn't want to go talk to them again.

He began having the mentality also of, "If you don't talk about it, it will go away".

It never did.

Even as Darvie became an adult, and he had tried to make himself think that the kidnapping never happened, I would gently try to tell him how important it was to talk about it. He would always disagree with me.

Eventually I stopped bringing it up to him for us to discuss.

I have heard it said that when bad things happen to someone at an early age, they have a hard time growing in maturity. Well Darvie always stayed having a childlike heart and mind.

I always said, "He was in his *thirties going on fourteen,* which was really true in a lot of ways."

However he had a memory that would beat anyone's. He could tell you what clothes someone had on years earlier, at a particular place we were. I could ask him a question about anyone that I had a hard time remembering, and he would with detail tell me all about them.

"You mean Mom, Mrs. *So and So* with the black car and the green house with the old dog that always barked in the backyard?"

It was amazing to listen to all that he remembered.

While in his teens, I could rely on him to go on walks with me. He was never embarrassed to be seen with me when his peers would drive by. He always seemed to be proud of me. It was like he wanted everyone to know that I was his mom.

I walked a mile or two daily for awhile. It was always nice to have someone to talk to when I did go on my walks. And, boy, did he talk! Neither one of us really ever had trouble finding things to say.

It has been so many years ago that we took those walks. I do not remember why, but Darvie and I used to talk so much that eventually we would end up in an argument. Then we would continue on our walk about twenty feet away from each other not saying a word to each other.

And the both of us were so stubborn, neither one of us wanted to make the first move. I don't know who it was that would eventually break the friction, but most likely it was him. Before I knew it, we were back walking side by side again continuing our talk. I know Darvie never wanted anything to come between us.

If it was a wedding out of town that I was going to or a trip to see an old friend, Darvie was always the one who went with me. One time right after Darvie had turned eleven I was going to go out of town to visit a girlfriend of mine overnight. Darvie had come with me, and we had gone out to eat at a Chinese restaurant for dinner.

I do not know what got it all started, but Darvie and I and my friend got the giggles so hard that we could not stop laughing. We cracked up so much, for so long, that many people in the restaurant started laughing also. It is such a great memory that I will always have.

In high school, he was liked by many of the girls. He always had to have his light brown hair *just right* and with it being a little long as the trend was back in the late 80s. Wearing the most popular clothes, he was known as one of the best-looking guys. He was carefree, and he always could make everyone laugh. He was a fun guy to be around. With the bussing jobs that he had worked at starting at an early age, he had been able to save his money, and so he also had the coolest cars that everyone wanted to drive around in.

He had a flamboyant personality and I think many guys his age were jealous of him because he always was able to charm the girls. He wasn't exceptionally tall in high school but he came across to the girls looking *real fine*.

Darvie was also a really hard worker.

When he wasn't doing as well as he could in school with his grades, Darvis and I let him make a decision that we have always regretted. We told him he could quit school if he wanted to. We were okay with it just as long as he continued to work at a job. What were we thinking?

Unfortunately, Darvie must have already started experimenting with drugs or soon afterward, because of the change in behavior that we started to see in him.

I think drugs helped him forget the past. He knew people who would give him drugs, and it was all part of the beginning of his downfall.

Without the goal of getting an education, it seemed every corner that Darvie turned, there was somebody out there trying to take advantage of him, his car, his money, and his time. He became very vulnerable with all the predators out there that he started to encounter.

He had grown into such a handsome man. He gave his all at whatever job he had. He could easily do more than his share, and most of the time he did. He had so much potential. He could have succeeded in whatever he wanted to do with his life.

No matter what things were about to happen in his future, no matter how hard our relationship was going to be weathered and tried and taken through the test in the years to come, Darvie always continued to have a love for me that gave me no doubt of how special I was to him. He truly was my biggest fan.

If only no one would have introduced him to drugs. If only he wouldn't have taken the bait, they had offered so freely.

Darvis and I as his parents began to feel so helpless. We did not do drugs and watching something take precedence over his life like it did, was so hard to watch at times.

With a desperate heart, all I could do was pray to the Lord to put a hedge of protection around Darvie. And protect him, he did!

There are so many times the good Lord got Darvie out of bad situations. Way more times than Darvis and I have ever known.

The Lord continually gave my son second chances.

Jeremiah 29:11 was the scripture that I had always claimed for Darvie.

> "For I know the plans I have for you," declares the Lord, "plans to prosper you and not to harm you, plans to give you hope and a future."

I knew that the Lord loved Darvie dearly, and it was the Lord that I put my trust in to keep him safe.

We had some rough times from then on. With him "on drugs," he and I never could get along.

I tried *tough love* which was hard for me at times to have boundaries that I knew I couldn't let him cross. I loved him with all my heart but I knew I loved him enough to not want to watch him slowly die either.

We would tell Darvie that he could not be around us on drugs. Then without us knowing it at the time, he would just get picked up by his, older so called friends, and they would take him away. They would act like they were helping him out, but we found out later, all they did was just give him more drugs.

It disgusts me when I think of all the people that were so far in their addiction that they just helped bring our son down more in his.

Darvie never could shake that "monkey off his back". He would do well for awhile and then without any notice, he was "out on the road" again. This went on for many years.

Eventually he would have minor traffic violations, and he would become well known in our county court system because of them. I always wanted the judge to make him go to rehab but it was never a requirement. He spent some time in jail, and, like everyone else it seems that are in jail, he had high hopes of doing well once he got out.

It was always short lived though.

Sometimes Darvis and I wished he *was* in jail because then we would at least know that he was safe, Darvis and I also worried that one day we would get a call that would say that the drug had taken his life.

Even as Darvie got older, people always seemed to use him. He would work so hard helping others in Columbia do cleanup around their yards or their rentals and hardly would get paid anything. His vehicles would get destroyed by using it to help others. We would get so frustrated hearing about people taking advantage of him. We would try to get him to not allow others to do that to him, but it seemed to be to no avail. He had a hard time speaking up and defending himself.

Darvis and I did not really know any of the people Darvie associated with in Columbia, but we always felt like many of them were doing him no good at all.

Feeling nothing but frustration, Darvis and I would try and put our foot down. We would tell Darvie that we could no longer help him unless he went and got some help for himself.

One time before we could enforce that, something happened that I will never forget.

Another six years had went by, and we had sold our place in Jamestown and had bought another home back in Sonora, this time not far from the town of Columbia.

We had a small travel trailer of ours parked next to our house, and we let Darvie live in it. One night he was in the trailer, and I went out to see him like I did often and knocked on the door. When I noticed that he wasn't coming to the door, I tried the door but it was locked. When I looked in through a slit in a curtain, I saw him sitting on the couch. It was apparent that he was unconscious, if not dead. Horrified, I ran to my house and told Darvis to call 911.

I got the extra key to the trailer, and then I quickly ran and unlocked the door. When I again saw Darvie in that state, I panicked. I ran right next door to our rental where a paramedic lived to see if he was at home. He was not but his wife was. She knew better than me of what to do. So she came with me and checked Darvie out. She was able to tell me that Darvie was squeezing her hand as she was holding his. I was so anxious and impatient as it seemed to take forever to even hear the sirens coming from the ambulance that had been dispatched.

I felt so helpless!

I was so afraid that my son was going to die!

As the ambulance arrived and seeing the paramedics move a lot slower than I had wanted them to, was so hard to watch, I knew that they were professionals and panicking was something they were taught never to do.

Darvie was put in the ambulance and sent to the hospital.

He ended up staying in the hospital for a couple of weeks and ended up getting a small part of his left lung removed. The doctor told me that Darvie also had a serious back infection caused by the drugs. The doctor told me personally, "If he does not quit the drugs, within a year he will be paralyzed."

To reduce the risk of more infection, Darvie had a port put into his chest.

A port (or portacath) is a small medical appliance that is installed beneath the skin. A catheter connects the port to a vein. Under the skin, the port has a septum through which medicine can be injected and blood samples can be drawn many times, usually with less discomfort for the patient than a more typical "needlestick". The port is usually inserted in the upper chest, just below the clavicle or collar bone, leaving the patient's hands free.

One good thing with Darvie being in the hospital was that the nurses and assistants did everything they could to explain to him how important it was for him to kick his drug habit. They genuinely seemed to care for him.

With his particular fun type of personality, he won everyone's heart. While he was in the hospital he dressed in street clothes.

He was well known for walking back and forth through the corridor all day long talking to whomever he could find. One time when I had been at the hospital visiting him, we were going down an elevator as he was walking *me* out. He introduced me to a maintenance man.

All I could think laughing to myself was, *Only my son would know the maintenance man's name!*

Once he got out of the hospital, he never went back and had the port in his chest taken out like he was supposed to. So he just lived with the port sticking out of his chest for many years.

One problem that people have is that after years of drug abuse, doctors almost have no choice but to prescribe prescription drugs to people to help offset their addiction. They need medicine to help them sleep so the nightmares don't come. They need medicine so that they don't *hear* "the voices".

I remember Darvie telling his best friend Kathy while he was talking to her on the phone when they were both adults, "My mom told me that whenever I start hearing things, to say "I rebuke you, satan, in the Name of Jesus!" It *really* works!"

He tried so hard to do whatever would work, to free him.

But many people coming off of drugs can't handle the responsibility of even taking prescription drugs correctly. They eventually learn how to abuse prescribed drugs too.

This is another thing that Darvie struggled with.

Sadly, it seemed that "normal" was just too much for him to bear.

So usually, it was when something like this happened and we would again express our concern to Darvie that he had to change his ways, he would decide to go to a rehab facility. He went a couple of times to try to get help but never stayed long.

He even tried Teen Challenge in Sacramento, California, and, actually, within a month, we could see a big difference in his behavior. He told us that he knew the Lord wanted him to live his life different from then on.

He used to tell me that he would see so many people in these drug rehab programs sneak around and somehow get drugs and do other things that they were not allowed to do.

I think the temptations got the best of Darvie and out of the program he would go.

He lived behind our house in his own travel trailer off and on for a few years after that. He had a girlfriend, and they saw each other for quite awhile. They had attended the same grammar school together. He truly loved her, but she just was not ready to make a more serious commitment. I know that Darvie always felt letdown after losing her.

Darvie had a wonderful Christian friend named Eleanor that lived in Oregon. He had met Eleanor many years earlier, and he and this elderly woman always e-mailed back and forth to each other. Eleanor was constantly helping him with her encouraging words to him. She gave him scripture after scripture to read and they would recite the twenty third Psalm over and over again together.

Eleanor believed in him and I think she kept him from going down the wrong path many times.

Darvie would do great for awhile, and then for no rhyme or reason even when things seemed to be going so well for him, he would relapse. It was so discouraging to us.

Darvis and I knew that we couldn't do it for him. I sure wish we could have.

Darvie always wanted to be accepted and loved by everyone. He tried in so many ways to make everyone happy.

In August 2008 when Darvie was thirty-four years old, he made headlines when he was up exploring in a mine on a mountain quite a ways above our property and fell down one hundred feet. He had slid sixty feet and fell forty more feet, landing in water and complete darkness.

We were not aware of anything until a guy kept driving back and forth on our road one morning and it made Darvis curious. The guy seemed to be looking for someone. My husband stopped him to ask him if he needed any help. The guy told him that he was with Darvie up on the mountain behind our property the night before looking around the mines that were up there. Darvie had gone inside one of the mines, but he was too afraid to go in them so he had stayed outside. Darvie hadn't come out of the mine by the time he had to leave. He had banged on the railroad tracks trying to see if Darvie would come out. When Darvie did not come out, he just thought that Darvie would just come out later on and walk back to his trailer.

When the guy came back in the morning to get Darvie because they were supposed to go on a job together, and Darvie wasn't in his trailer, he started to worry.

So the guy left to get help from Darvie's friend, Kevin. Kevin was familiar with the mines and wasn't afraid to go in them. A short while later, the two guys came back and Kevin went in the mine. He kept calling for Darvie and finally he heard Darvie way down below. When he came back out, he said Darvie was asking for me.

The relief Darvis and I felt when we found out that Darvie had been found was again the sweet comfort that we had experienced over twenty years earlier when he had been kidnapped and then found.

Thankful to the Lord, we then began to deal with the situation at hand.

At this point, Darvie had been in complete darkness for nineteen hours—only Darvie and God in complete silence.

I do not know how Darvie withstood the nightmare of falling down a mine and being trapped there so far below. I know I wouldn't have been able to make it through, even emotionally.

To know that my son was so far down in a mine was unbelievable. He was at a place where man doesn't even go.

I wanted him out of there as quick as we could get him out. When Kevin had found him, he had tried to go down on a ladder to reach Darvie in the darkness, but when he did, one side of the ladder had broken, and Kevin had injured his leg really bad. Darvis had asked Kevin to drop down to Darvie one of his good heavy flashlights. It quickly was lost in the water, but not until it hit Darvie in the head on its way down in the darkness.

I was so thankful that Darvie had not been knocked unconscious by the hit to his head. A miracle!

Kevin talked of getting a long rope down to Darvie. Knowing how dangerous it all was, we knew that we could not have Kevin now risking his life.

I did not know how we were going to get him out so we then called the Tuolumne County Sheriff's Department.

They had the local search and rescue team come out, and Kevin showed them where Darvie was. The team was able to use a cable with a basket attached to it to take down some hot soup and hot chocolate that I had fixed for Darvie after they had asked me to prepare it for him. They also sent down another flashlight. This one Darvie was able to retrieve from the basket. They were able to talk with Darvie, and they could hear him faintly down below answering them.

The search and rescue team tried to get down to Darvie, but when they realized that it was too dangerous trying to reach him and beyond their expertise, they had to call out another team from Los Angeles, California.

The only problem we had was once our county gave the jurisdiction to another county they would not let anyone else go back into the mine. Darvis and I asked the officer-in-charge to *please* have at least someone go back in and tell Darvie that help was on the way so that he would know that. The officer refused to allow anyone back in. So when Darvis started to go himself into the mine to tell Darvie, he was quickly brought back out with the knowledge that he would be arrested if he tried to go back in again.

I begged Darvis to not go back in.

I knew that when Darvie eventually came out he would need us both and we couldn't risk Darvis getting in trouble.

It was all so confusing. I felt like if it had been a child that had fallen down in the mine, surely they would have had someone up above reassuring them "the whole time" that they would be okay.

To not even let Darvie know what was going on did not seem fair at all. To not even tell Darvie that though he would not hear back from anyone for awhile, we were still nearby waiting, seemed almost cruel.

Unbeknownst to us, it was going to take "five more hours" for the other search and rescue team to arrive and be ready to go down and rescue Darvie. They were coming from Los Angeles, California by helicopter to a nearby airport in Columbia.

If Darvis or I would have known that it was actually going to take that long, I know nothing would have stopped us from trying to go back into the mine. We would have been frantic wanting to let Darvie know how much longer he would have to wait.

I am thankful again to the Lord that we did not have that foresight because neither one of us would have wanted to be arrested.

Darvie later told us that while he was down in the mine he felt like he was going in and out of consciousness. He kept thinking that he had just been dreaming when someone had talked with him earlier. He had a hard time separating reality from fantasy. He kept feeling like the water inside where he was, was rising. Before he had received the flashlight, he said he could see absolutely nothing and only sat on the edge of a ledge yet constantly would slip down in the cold water only to reach into the darkness to try to get back up on the ledge. He blindly sought for anything that would keep him above the water.

It sounded like such a nightmare to me.

The search and rescue team were very professional and did everything that they knew to prepare everyone that was going down in the mine. As a parent, again watching everything go by so slowly just as I had four years earlier waiting on the ambulance to arrive, to take Darvie to the hospital, was so frustrating for me. I wanted to see them rushing around as quickly as they could to get to my son, but I knew that they needed to take their time to get it all done safely.

I couldn't imagine what Darvie was doing down there.

Darvis and I were so afraid that the mine might collapse on top of him. The search and rescue team said that there was a chance of that happening. We knew that we could only trust that the Lord would keep Darvie safe.

We had some family members come by to give us some moral support during the ordeal which was very much appreciated.

The search team risked their lives and later the next day, they brought him and everyone else out of the mine safely. I will always be forever grateful to them.

It was a total of thirty-four hours from the time Darvie fell down in the mine to the time Darvie was brought up to safety.

As soon as Darvie was brought out of the mine, as if he was back to being a little boy, he called out for me. All he wanted was his dad and me.

He hardly had any scrapes on him. It truly was amazing!

Darvie had said that while he was down in the mine shaft, he had a heart-to-heart talk with the Lord and he knew he had to change the direction that his life was going in again.

Many times throughout his life Darvie had gotten himself in bad predicaments. Sometimes by his own doings. But he never deserved to have anybody do harm to him, whatever it was they did.

Darvie always trusted everyone. He wanted to always believe the best in others. He had a kind heart, and he wouldn't have hurt anyone intentionally. He was the kind of person that you could tell anything to. But he was so bad at keeping secrets. He may never have kept your secret for very long. However he was someone you would want to talk to about anything though, regardless.

That is one of the hardest things that I have had to accept since he went missing, is not having him to talk to.

I'm sure there are so many others that knew Darvie that feel the same way.

Darvie really had a problem with people who told lies, and so even in his life he tried to be as honest as much as he could. If he told me something, that he felt I should know, but he had failed to tell me everything, it wasn't long afterward that I would get the "whole" story.

For awhile his life would begin to get better. He knew the right way to live, and he really tried to stay away from anyone who could be a bad influence.

Darvie and I would have so much fun at times. If it was taking kids to the waterslides or just going out to eat somewhere or stopping at the grocery store for a moment to get a few things, he could get me laughing so hard. It always felt good to laugh with him. He was a lot of fun.

I even went with him to Celebrate Recovery a few times. Celebrate Recovery is a Christian-based twelve-step program to help people overcome their hurts, habits, and hang-ups. Darvie went to Celebrate Recovery for his drug addiction, and I went to support him.

Darvie even got me involved to help feed the hungry a Thanksgiving meal one year at a local church's yearly event. He had us both dishing out food for the people. I enjoyed doing that with him.

Darvie eventually got the port in his chest removed. To him it was such an eyesore and had no longer been needed since he had gotten out of the hospital a few years earlier.

He finally got himself some prescription glasses so that he could see better and even went and got himself fitted for dentures since his teeth had been destroyed from the drug abuse. Constantly eating raw sugar like he did and drinking lots of Pepsi for so many years did not help the situation either.

Growing up, Darvie had always been someone who took pride in the way he looked, but the drugs took all that away from him.

Eventually, the struggle was just too hard for him again, and old acquaintances were always more than willing to bring him back down to the bottom where they were.

Darvis and I then confronted Darvie again about the direction that he was going with his life. We told him that he had to make some decisions because we could no longer watch his downfall.

Shortly afterward one night he accidentally went over an embankment in his truck. Darvie survived that without a scrape. He had totaled his truck. That truck really was one of the last good things Darvie felt that he had going for him.

The next day, he took me to where he had gone off the road. He wanted to show me how far down it was to where his truck had landed.

No one would be able to believe that he made it out alive if they did not see it for themselves.

This was again another miracle from God.

I think the realization of knowing that he had just lost one of his last prized possessions, being his fairly new Toyota Tundra, it didn't take Darvie long to run to the vice that helped him try to ignore the reality of it all.

So in the drug-induced condition he was in a few days after he wrecked his truck, we were forced to call a friend of ours that was a pastor. We didn't know if we should call the cops because of his behavior or take him to the hospital.

Darvie wouldn't open the door for anyone, but then when our friend arrived and he told Darvie that I wanted him to open the door, he did. We all told him that he was going to go to the hospital because we knew that something was wrong with him.

Again the nurses and the assistants really showed him how much they cared about him. They let him know that he was important enough to get clean. Some of them he had even went to school with.

Darvie was told, if we took him back home, in a few days he would have to go into a rehab facility *or* move his trailer off of our property. He knew that we were really serious this time.

It didn't take him long to know that he had to stop the madness.

Darvis and I knew we had to move quickly.

So within a few days we got everything set up, and we took him to a Salvation Army Rehab Center in Fresno, California. It seemed like a great place for him to get well.

But it didn't take long and before we knew it, he had contacted some old acquaintances of his that lived in the city where he was going to rehab. To me, these people had never been anything but trouble for him. I was sure things were not going to be any better this time around either.

Darvie began telling me that he knew that he could come out of the program and kick the habit all on his own. We tried to encourage him to stay in the program.

He lasted only three weeks and then ended up leaving.

Unfortunately Darvie hooked back up with those old acquaintances that I felt had always been a bad influence for him to be around. They were people I had never had anything to do with because I always believed that they were part of the cause of his early addiction. It looked to me like they had only encouraged his addiction in the past because Darvie had told me many years later that these *older so-called friends* gave him drugs early on as well as did the drugs with him.

His dad and I were so bummed out. We felt like our hands were tied. Then a short time later, he shocked us all and told us that he was going to get married. We felt like he was making a mistake. We were so afraid of the bad influences that we felt some of his old acquaintances had always been on him. We truly wanted him to be happy so we ended up supporting him 100 percent regardless, as he was making one of the biggest decisions of his life.

He was now going to be a stepdad, but also the main father figure to two young children.

I think for the next year or so, it was being "Dad" to them that kept him trying to stay on the right track.

He tried to bring as much "normalcy" as he could to them and give them a good life. He tried to show them how much he loved them.

Darvie had always wanted to be a Dad and he hoped to have his own son one day that would carry on his name.

He moved to Oregon and he eventually went back to school. He also got a job as a groundskeeper for the same college he was attending. He seemed to be doing well. At least, he seemed to be doing a lot better than he had been doing in the recent past.

I even made two trips up to Oregon to see him and his new family. One time I surprised him early on Thanksgiving and the next time it was the beginning of summer, only four months before strange turn of events would start to take place.

Things started falling apart in his marriage. Before Darvie would have a chance to file a restraining order of his own that he had already started the paperwork on, he was slapped with two restraining orders and forced to leave his home. He was given no warning. A police officer came to his door, served him the papers, and told him that he had to get out of the house right then and there.

Darvie called me so upset. He did not know what to do. He was now going to be homeless. He had nowhere to stay up there. He was now going to be forced to leave his good job and quit school.

My husband and I knew he could not stay up there anymore.

Since things were now getting so bad, he had to get out of there. We encouraged him to come back to California.

Darvie had a few hours before he would be allowed to go back to his home to get his belongings. So he went and got a monthly pay-as-you-go plan back on his phone.

As he waited to be able to go back to his home, he wrote a list of important things that he wanted to make sure that he got, once he got back into the house.

Unfortunately when Darvie returned back to his home to get his possessions, the local authorities did not give him very much time at all to collect his things. It seemed all so unfair.

To me, what he brought back with him to California was worth more in sentimental value than anything he could have left behind, because it was things that were tender to his heart. Some of the things he had even kept since his childhood.

We have never had the rest of our son's belongings returned to us.

With this sudden turn of events, it brought new stress to our lives. I was so afraid for the past to repeat itself, but Darvis and I definitely wanted Darvie to come back here to Sonora since he had nowhere else to go. It was all just happening too fast. We didn't even have time to think of what was the best move for him.

Even a God-ordained meeting took place between Darvie and his sister Kristie. They had not been able to see each other for quite awhile because of how far they lived apart.

But Kristie happened to be at our house dropping off our granddaughters for the weekend which was a rare event, when Darvie had made the call to me from Oregon.

A few days later when Kristie came back to pick up her girls to take them home she had a nice visit with her brother, not knowing that it was the last time they would ever see each other.

Darvis and I also never realized at the time that by coming back here, Darvie was coming back once again to more bad influences.

And we did not know the plans that others would begin to make that would take his life in only seventeen days.

4

Many have thought that Darvie was having so many bad things happen to him because he continued in his addiction, and., yes, he did make that choice. Some have even had little compassion for his rough road that he traveled due at times by his own mistakes and choices, but I tell you that no one starts out wanting to be a drug addict.

Over eleven million people have tried methamphetamine for the first time. The drug has a high potential for abuse. It is highly addictive and toxic to the brain. '*Meth*' can give you a high that can damage your body and brain for life. It may lead to severe psychological or physical dependence because it is a drug that quickly pulls you in and for the millions of people who haven't been strong enough to walk away, it destroys your life.

Life is never what God intended for you when you decide to take that plunge, sometimes only just once.

That is why I try to tell children and young adults, *"Please don't even try drugs!"*

So with the knowledge of knowing firsthand what this drug had already done to our family, and for Gloria to come to our home and talk to us about what she thought happened to Darvie was real concerning to me.

Tuesday, October 26, 2010—Continued

As we left our house to go meet up with Detective Bob, Darvis and I took Gloria with us in our truck so we could talk with her. Right away, I felt a bond with her. Gloria's husband and friend followed behind in their vehicle. We only had to drive a few miles away to wait for the detective in the nearby town of Columbia.

It took the detective quite awhile to arrive since he wanted some people from our local search and rescue team to come along with us. That took extra time.

The waiting was hard. I wanted to get to Darvie as quickly as I could.

I just kept thinking he had gotten himself hurt and was probably under some kind of shelter, waiting to be rescued.

I felt so anxious.

If only we would have found out this information sooner...

While we were waiting in our vehicle, Gloria began to tell us how she knew Darvie.

She said she had known Darvie since he was in high school. Even though she was a few years older than him, they became friends through other acquaintances. He always seemed to be around to help her in many ways. One time, he even helped move her and her family when they were relocating to another home. Gloria said Darvie was a good person, and they cared about each other a lot. She said that they used to have fun and joke around all the time together.

Gloria said since he had been back up here for these seventeen days, she had only seen him once when she had stopped over at Debby's house, which was just days before.

Even though she knew that Darvie and Debby had problems with each other in the past, she did not think much about him being there. However, Gloria did say that she mentioned to Debby, "You better not be the *downfall* of Darvie".

Gloria said that Darvie had always said, "Debby would be the death of me."

While Gloria was over at Debby's house, Darvie told Gloria about his stepchildren and how much he loved them.

He said it was the kids that he missed the most.

He showed her pictures of them that he had on his cell phone.

She said Darvie told her about all the trouble that was going on up in Oregon. He also told her that there were people up there that wanted him *"Dead off the face of the earth"*.

We found out later, that there is a connection between Mark and Debby and some of the people in Oregon that go way back. It seems like some kind of a crazy triangle.

It had now gotten dark when the detective finally showed up. Gloria stayed with us in our vehicle and told us where to go.

The drive took us about ten miles away, and it seemed to take forever as we traveled a winding road leading us to the top of the highest mountain to the turnoff.

Once we arrived at the top of the mountain, we traveled down a narrow dirt road. It took us all the way out in the boonies. A place we had never been before.

There were four other vehicles that followed behind us. Gloria's husband and friend were in one vehicle, and the other three vehicles were law enforcement and the search and rescue team.

Eventually wood limbs were sticking out on each side of the road and it made it difficult to not get our vehicle scratched as we drove by. The dirt road was very bumpy.

On our drive there, I was so anxious to find Darvie. The darkness, made it difficult to make out where we were going. It was all so unfamiliar to me.

Gloria was watching out for a particular old tree for a landmark that would tell her that we were almost at the destination that we were searching for. Gloria said that the tree looked very creepy and she felt that if only the tree could talk…the things that it would say.

We relied totally on her to get us to the right place. I just wanted to reach our destination as quickly as we could. I too felt like we did not have much time.

The darkness seemed to press in all around us as we finally arrived at an entrance to a dirt driveway. Hardly anyone would have been able to see it from the road. If you didn't know that there was a dirt driveway there, you would most likely just pass it by.

After we all got out of our vehicles, Gloria, her husband, and friend said they were leaving. They said they would let us check out the property alone with the Tuolumne County Sheriff's Department.

Gloria said that the place just gave her *the willies*.

We thanked them, and they went home.

Ever since Gloria told us what Mark had said about the landowner, all I kept thinking of was about this *crazy* landowner.

I also kept thinking that we needed to be careful and watch out for him. Every step we took, I kept expecting him to suddenly appear with a gun.

With flashlights in hand, we started down the driveway.

We walked about one hundred feet and then we came upon a big green iron gate.

On it in big red letters were painted the words:

"Keep the *F——* out."

"You will hurt."

"You will bleed."

What! You will *bleed*!?

Did I read that right?

You will bleed?

I was horrified!

I kept thinking, *Who writes such things?*

But what I could not understand was what I was seeing, was worse than even the words that I was reading.

Hanging down from the gate, tied together right in the middle of all the words, was our son's new work boots that he had just bought!

5

Tuesday, October 26, 2010—Continued

We all quickly walked up to observe the brand new work boots hanging down in the center of the gate. The boots were tied together and had some burrs on them. The detective took the boots down. We knew that they were Darvie's because Darvie had just bought the same brand of boots a few days earlier. The boot box that the boots had came in, was still at our house in the room that he was staying in.

The gate was locked so we had to figure out how to get around it. On one side of the gate there was barbed wire and on the other side there was a wooden box. We all stepped up on the wooden box and climbed over.

There was around five or six of us, so it took awhile for us all to climb over safely.

We walked about twenty-five yards, and the light of the flashlights revealed to us that we were coming up to a bulldozer. This bulldozer also had some spray-painted words on the blade.

As our flashlights moved over the bulldozer, we read, "Keep the F——Out" and "You will hurt" in letters about twelve inches high.

It was so unbelievable to me.

Knowing someone had supposedly left Darvie out there and now reading these words, it made me start worrying about what could have happened to him. However, I did not want to go there in my mind, so I just pushed that thought away. Before we had come to this property, I had thought of Darvie being left out here and possibly getting himself hurt somehow that made him incapable of getting out. I was thinking he was waiting desperately for someone to come rescue him.

Even with law enforcement with us, the only fear I had was being encountered by a *crazy* landowner. A *crazy* landowner that was capable of writing such things as those words.

We walked two hundred yards more down a dirt road. The road had been cut in the mountain by a dozer probably years ago.

We came upon a couple of rundown weathered trailers that were connected to each other inside. The siding was coming off in many different areas on the outside of both.

We opened the door to one of the trailers and stepped inside.

The trailers were filthy inside and it was obvious that no one had actually lived in them for a long time. Many empty containers of canned food lay around everywhere. There were several sets of eyeglasses found in a cupboard. Trash and debris were just about in every spot that you looked. Small miscellaneous household items had been left there for many years it seemed, and then through all the years of neglect, they became filthy and destroyed.

There was an old mattress in one of the trailers and a small couch in the other one. Rat feces were everywhere.

One item that really stood out to me was a pillar candle. It had been placed on a paper plate at one time and left on the floor. It had also been lit and had burnt down to almost nothing.

After checking the trailers out, we continued walking.

Everything was going at such a slower pace than I wanted to go.

I wanted to find Darvie! But just where was he?

We passed an old Ford Courier dump bed truck and a rusty flatbed trailer.

Within fifty feet, we came upon a pair of jeans with a belt in them lying on the ground next to the edge of a bank. The detective picked up the jeans and inside one of the pockets were Darvie's car key on the Hawaii keychain that I had given him so many years before. In the other pants pocket was the lid and the top part cut off from a tube of the denture cream that Darvie always used.

As I looked at the jeans, I thought I recognized them and I thought they must be the new jeans that Darvie had just bought.

Detective Bob picked up the jeans. He said that they were kind of damp all over. He was wondering how that could have happened.

I just thought that the jeans were most likely damp from just being out in the elements.

The jeans did not seem dirty at all, but they had a tear in them, in the back toward the top. I thought at the time that it looked like a tear someone would get if they had caught it on something like a barbedwire fence.

We continued walking about twenty-five yards, and then we came upon a mine.

There close to the entrance, a brand new white sock was lying on the ground. The detective picked it up.

Then some of the search and rescue people that were with us went inside the mine. When they came out, they had found nothing.

We kept calling for Darvie. We were yelling out his name just in case he could hear us, wherever he was, but it was so dark outside. We all knew that we would have to wait until morning to come back again. Then we would be able to see things better.

There had not been any rain recently. The weather was actually pretty nice. Because it was so dark, we did not notice the moon at all. It must have been way over on the other side of the sky, hidden by the mountains and the tall trees.

Walking back past the old truck, we looked inside the cab this time and spotted something that we had not noticed the first time walking past it.

Inside the cab, another brand new white sock rolled up a bit, was lying on the seat.

To me it seemed like the sock had been carelessly thrown in there.

In fact, it looked to me like all of Darvie's clothes had been planted by someone.

Placed there by a person other than Darvie and meant to be eventually found.

I felt so helpless. I did not know what else we could do to find him in the dark. Law enforcement wanted to leave and come back the next day.

Wherever my son was, I sure hoped he was going to be okay.

With heavy hearts, Darvis and I went home.

We found out later that Mark had been in trouble with the law a few months earlier, shortly after he was released from prison, and the Tuolumne County Sheriff's Department had actually chased him out to this very location where we discovered our son's clothing and boots. Mark had been able to ditch the officers and ended up here with his truck on fire from an overheated engine at the top of this very road. Mark had since been on the run from the local police.

Later, we also heard through some acquaintances of Darvie's that Mark had been hanging out here for the past few months. Mark had even been heard saying that his grandfather actually owned the property, which we later found out to be a lie. These acquaintances also told us that Mark had even stayed in the rundown trailers on this property.

Wednesday, October 27, 2010

On this morning, Darvis, Bobby, Kristie, and I followed Detective Bob and a few other officers, and headed back up to the property where Darvie's clothes and boots were found.

I was confused about who owned the property and who owned the mines. I thought they were two different people, and I thought that the landowner lived nearby or actually on the property. The detective cleared it up and informed me that the landowner also owned the mines and did not live near the property but instead lived in town.

The sheriff's office had located a man with his hound dog, trained to track scents to possibly locate a person who was lost. He was going to come out and meet us up there with his hound dog and try to help search the property along with our local search and rescue team.

Darvis, Bobby, Kristie and I were asked to stay behind the gate while they searched.

We had no problem waiting at first, but after awhile, we went over the gate and just stood maybe one hundred feet from it, anxiously waiting. There was a lot of territory to cover so we knew that it could take awhile.

I was just waiting for someone to run up and tell us that they had found Darvie and that he was okay and that they were bringing him up to us.

We were there quite awhile as was expected, and eventually everybody including the search and rescue team started coming back up. Sadly, Darvie was not with them. The team said that they had seen two or three other mines on the property, but after exploring inside them, they had found nothing in them.

The hound dog had not found anything either but the search and rescue team had found a shirt over by a boat that was by a mine entrance. The shirt was a little dirty and had some burrs on it just like the boots had. We believed that it was probably

Darvie's. They also showed us a sweatshirt that they had found behind the two trailers that had the name of the college that Darvie had been attending and working at. My heart was broken.

The sweatshirt was found further back up the road from where all the other items were found, and it was down an embankment about fifty feet.

The sweatshirt and the keychain were one of the most heartbreaking pieces of items to me that were found. It represented to me an absolute truth that it was our son's belongings.

These items had gotten here on this property. But *how?*

The sweatshirt was something that Darvie had proudly worn since he had worked and went to school at that college, and the keychain he had always admired. They were priceless to me.

Sometimes I think if Darvie had really been on this property, for sure, that he might have taken the sweatshirt off and left it down there, and no one, even the person who seemed to have planted the clothes, ever really knew that it was there at all. Then the search and rescue team had seen it and went and retrieved it.

I will always believe that it is possible that the other article of clothes that were found were originally left at Debby's house and brought later to this property, probably after we picked up Darvie's car since his car key was in the jeans pocket, and placed there by someone, possibly by Mark, and that Darvie still had other clothes on when something happened to him.

For some reason though the hound dog had wanted to go back up on the road from where we started from, but not much more was done, and eventually we all left the area.

Where was Darvie?

I had thought that he would have been found by now. This was getting so hard to believe that this nightmare was becoming our reality.

After we left that area, Darvis and I, and Kristie and Bobby didn't follow everyone out. Instead, we went up on some land that Gloria had told us about that had a helicopter pad just a few miles away from the property and as soon as we walked up to it, we spotted two plastic gas cans across the area by some bushes.

We walked over to where the gas cans were and realized that one of the gas cans had the name Eric written on it.

Eric was the name of Debby's ex husband.

We already knew from talking to people that we were starting to encounter that Mark had carried plastic gas cans in the back of his truck.

With us knowing the gas purchase that had just been made with Darvie's ATM card at the mini-mart almost a week earlier, the gas cans seemed just big enough to fill up the little over $17.00 worth of gas that was purchased.

Right beside the gas cans, we found an *Army* shirt that we just knew was Darvie's shirt, because Darvis had given Darvie a shirt just like it, and it was the same size.

I started to think that we were on to something, like we were getting closer to finding him.

Darvis quickly called Detective Bob, who had already arrived back to his office by then and told him what we had found. He said that he would come right out to where we were.

My heart was so heavy though. I wanted everything to "hurry up and get over with". I wanted Darvie found safely and then all this madness would end.

There were two piles of garbage that had been dumped on this property. Each pile consisted of different garbage items, but one pile had been partially burned in a burn pile. None of the piles had any food items in them, so it wasn't raw garbage.

We all looked through the first garbage pile briefly but found nothing out of the ordinary, but we did find a brand new pair of men's underwear that had never been worn and tossed out in the pile. It just made me wonder whose it was. I knew that Darvie had just recently purchased a whole bunch of things at our local Walmart so everything that I saw made me curious if any of it was his.

We then went and started checking out the burnt garbage pile.

Kristie and I began to smell something dead in the air that we believed to be a dead animal smell, but we could not figure out where it was coming from. So we started digging with some sticks around the burnt garbage pile scratching only the surface, but again came up with nothing. The odor just seemed to be flowing though the air, away from where we were. We walked over and looked through a bunch of bushes but did not find anything.

There were also shotgun shells everywhere which made me wonder why that would be? But Darvis said that many of the shells were old casings and that people probably came up there all the time and did target shooting.

The embankments to the side of where the gas cans and the *Army* shirt had been found were very steep. We tried going down the embankment a little ways but then realized that it would just be too dangerous to attempt going down any further without some kind of a cable holding us securely as we made our way down.

As soon as Detective Bob arrived, he took the gas cans and the *Army* shirt and took them down to the Tuolumne County Sheriff's Office.

I began to worry that Darvie might be somewhere, being held against his will. I knew that Halloween was going to be here within just a few days and since I had heard that Debby dabbled in the occult, if something had not already happened to Darvie, I was so frightened that something would. It was the worse feeling that I had ever felt before.

All I could do was cry out to the Lord. I knew he was the only one who could help us.

Trying to figure out though why we were not being able to locate him was very confusing to me.

Feeling horribly helpless, we went back home.

Kristie and Bobby decided to spend the night and we made plans to go out again the next day.

Thursday, October 28, 2010

Early in the morning, we went and picked Gloria and her husband up.

At first Gloria took us up to some abandoned trailers where a friend of hers used to live. The place with its broken windows was filled with trash inside and out. Lots of furniture was thrown over embankments and everywhere you looked was filth. Forgotten toys, clothes, and shoes, broken or just soiled, were everywhere you looked.

It was so hard for us to believe that people had even lived in rundown places such as this. It was not anything that we were used to seeing.

We looked around but again came up with nothing.

We then left and drove up to the helicopter pad again.

We also found a part to Mark's truck up there that Gloria knew was his. We looked thoroughly through the garbage again.

In one of the piles after doing a better search of it, we found papers with Debby's name on it.

In the burn pile while looking through some plastic bags, we also found one of Debby's cats that had died that Gloria recognized. It had been put in a plastic bag and not even properly buried.

That made Kristie and I think that the dead animal smell that we had smelt the day before had been just that.

We tried to check out everything even more. Then we left the area.

Nothing was making sense. I was so discouraged.

I knew God could do anything for us.

I just didn't want to have to go through this.

I wondered why this was all happening, but I never doubted God. I knew he could be trusted regardless of what was happening around us.

We then dropped off Gloria and her husband back at their house.

Afterward for some reason, we had wanted to stop by the Tuolumne County Sheriff's Office to talk with Detective Bob some more, even though we knew that the next day the sheriff's office would be bringing out more dogs to search the area and we would see him then.

But after we arrived at the sheriff's office knowing that the doors would be locked, Darvis called the detective to let him know that we were there. He asked us to wait in our truck.

For some reason, Bobby had gotten out of our vehicle and was standing on the other side talking to Darvis at the driver's window.

As we were waiting for the detective, we noticed a man coming out and leaving from inside the building. He was walking over to get to his truck that was parked right next to us. But then he turned toward our truck and while Bobby was still on the other side of our vehicle, the man stuck his hand through the open window on the passenger's side to my husband who was in the driver's seat, and introduced himself to Darvis, saying that he was Chuck our neighbor that lived right down the road from us.

We did not think anything about it until the detective came out and told us that the man who had just left in his vehicle was indeed the landowner of the property where we were searching for Darvie and where his clothes and boots had been found.

The landowner?

Bobby and I both said right then and there that we couldn't believe such a man that came across so passive, was in fact the same man capable of writing such horrible, aggressive words on a gate and bulldozer and then admitting it to the local sheriff's department that he had written them.

And what I kept thinking was, 'Why did he have a cut on his forehead'?

6

Oh, how my heart yearned to find my son.

I used to go outside at night after that first week that we knew he was missing and think of him. As the weather was starting to cool down, I was so afraid that Darvie was out in the elements somewhere. I wanted so desperately to find him and bring him in, out of the cold.

I couldn't stop thinking that he was being held against his will somewhere.

I was terrified that someone had taken him away and would never let him go.

One time one of my younger sons called out to me on their way upstairs and just for a second...The voice sounded just like Darvie's and I thought for a moment that it was him.

We called our local newspaper and asked them to please let our community know that we were offering a $10,000 reward to anyone who could lead us to Darvie.

We set up a fund at a local bank and asked anyone who felt inclined to, could give contributions to help us in our search for our son and to contribute toward a reward if we ever needed to pay out one.

Getting flyers printed constantly, treating people that were helping us out to a meal, paying for gas for others who were helping us out that didn't have much, could become a financial hardship for us as the days could turn into months or even years, as we went searching for our son.

At one point I was calling the fund 1,000 for $10.00. If 1,000 people would just give $10.00, we would have our reward. Many people contributed to our fund, and, though, we didn't quite make it to the top, it helped us out in so many ways.

I will forever be grateful to each and every individual that saw us through, as we were forced to handle the ongoing nightmare.

For the next couple of weeks, new tips continued to come in to the sheriff's office. The tips came in almost on a daily basis. Detective Bob was investigating everything that he possibly could regarding Mark and Debby.

For the first few weeks it seemed Darvis, Kristie, Bobby, and I would drive and go up to the property, at least every other day to search where Darvie's clothes and boots had been found.

We had gone to our county courthouse and other businesses in town to check out maps of the area to try to locate where certain mines were located.

As the tips came in, Darvis was talking to the detective every day. With each new tip, it gave us more encouragement that we were eventually going to get the answers that we so desperately needed.

With me knowing so many people from so many walks of life, I continued getting tips on my own constantly. Many times the information that I received was new information to the sheriff's office or what I brought to them, they had just heard themselves. With me doing my own investigation, many things were brought to light.

Since Kristie and Bobby lived so far away, and they also had a family to tend to and jobs that they were expected to be at, when they couldn't come, Darvis and I continued our search alone.

With us living so much closer to the site, and, with me, working my job at home doing foster care and Darvis being retired, it gave us more opportunity to be able to go.

However, our granddaughters came up with Kristie and Bobby often and the support that we received from our places of work, and with our immediate family and friends volunteering to babysit, etc. was priceless.

I know that the Lord provided for us during that time. I do not know what we would have done if we would not have been able to go search as much as we were able to. The emotional strain that was on us all was almost too much to bear. Being able to feel like we were doing something to try to find Darvie gave us purpose. At least we were trying to do *something right*.

The Tuolumne County Sheriff's Department had already had a helicopter come out to the property and search from above. Men on ATVs and horses were also sent out to comb the area, but nothing more had been found.

Plans were then made to have a search dog team from a nearby county come out to help us search.

The search dog team had specialty trained cadaver dogs. They were specifically trained for Human Remains Detection or HRD.

So on November 11, 2010 the sheriff's department got the search dog team (HRD team) together, and they brought their two cadaver dogs to have them check out a few different areas.

The first area that the dogs searched at was at the helicopter pad. Our team—the Tuolumne County Sheriff's Department, the HRD team, Darvis, Bobby, Kristie, and I met at the site. The dogs went up and around the whole area quickly, but they did not pick up on anything.

Since the one side of the mountain where the helicopter pad is located was so steep, it also made it impossible for the dogs to climb down that far as a canyon is way down below.

After the helicopter site was searched, the team traveled to the property where Darvie's clothes and boots had been found.

The mines were checked again.

Around one particular mine where water flowed out continually, one of the dogs kept acting a little different. This was the lower mine that was closest to the rushing water creek below.

Kristie was with that half of the HRD team at the time and she was able to talk with the team and listen to any concerns that they may have had while they were in the area. But even though the dog had acted a little differently, it still did not give us any of the answers we needed.

We had been told by the sheriff's department that the creek had already been combed over real good by the first search and rescue team and the hound dog that had first came out.

The terrain was pretty rough and even though it was maybe only about one hundred yards below the lower mine to reach the bottom of the mountain, it would have taken awhile for us to get down there. We would have all went down there, but because we had been reassured that the area below had been searched by the first search and rescue team, none of us went down below the lower mine or even close to the water's edge.

Next, when all of the HRD team got back up to the top of the road again, one of the dogs and part of the team headed upward above the property. The other dog and the other part of the team, headed another way.

Up toward the top of the mountain somewhere, we knew lived an old hermit man named Henry who was friends with Chuck the landowner. Henry's place was the only home out there among all the forest.

Earlier in the day, Henry had driven by us heading to town and stopped and asked us, "Did you catch him yet?"

I had thought at the time that asking such a question sounded very strange to me.

This is one of the main reasons that I was encouraged to go up toward the old man's property.

Did he know something we didn't know?

Could he be trusted at all?

My family and I decided to follow the dog and the team that were going up the mountain.

The dog that we were with continued to want to climb up higher all the time, and so we continued doing just that.

I just felt like we were on a mission. We were doing all that we knew to do, and I was so hopeful that Darvie would be found as we searched in every building and rundown place that we saw on our search.

We climbed up such steep terrain that day. As unfit as Darvis and I are, we kept up with everyone else and for us to have been able to climb like we did was really amazing.

Eventually at a ridge on the mountain, the team that we were with, split up into two different groups. So Detective Bob, Darvis, Bobby, and I went off together. Kristie separated from us and went with the other group.

We eventually ended up on some other people's property. At one point we felt like we were getting lost. The sun was starting to go down, but then by us continuing around and down, we finally ended up on Henry's property. We were all so exhausted and had found nothing.

Henry's place is really on an old mining camp. It appears to look like a small hunting cabin out in nowhere land. There are a couple of old rusty vehicles laying around on the property. Piles of junk are everywhere. There is no electricity that far out and a wood stove is the only thing used for heat. A generator is used to give Henry phone service so that he can call out to anyone from his base phone.

To get to Henry's cabin by vehicle, you have to have four-wheel drive to get up his dirt road. The road is so bumpy. It is hard to believe that anyone would live up there so far away from civilization.

There are about a half a dozen peacocks that live on Henry's property so when they make their sound, it really is the only thing you ever hear. Otherwise, the place is just too quiet and desolate.

There were also a few mines on Henry's property, but not one was checked out.

To this day, not one of them ever has been searched.

I wanted Henry's mines checked out. I wanted to find my son, but no one but Kristie and I really felt the need to do that, and we were always told that those mines were really unsafe. There was a door at the opening of one of the mines, but it was shut tight. Darvis said that you could tell it hadn't been opened in years.

At the end of the day, I felt so discouraged because how did anyone know that Darvie wasn't in one of the mines up on this property?

How would we ever know?

Before the HRD team left, they mentioned that they would like to come out again sometime and search even higher toward the left of Henry's property. It gave me a little bit of hope.

The HRD team was now ready to leave the property. The sheriff's office asked them if before they left to go back home if their dogs could check out around those two abandoned trailers a few miles away off the main road where Gloria had taken us before and also over around the area by Debby's house and neighborhood. They said that they would.

For some reason we did not go with them and later we were told that the dogs picked up on nothing.

Even though the HRD team had mentioned wanting to come out again, it wasn't until almost a year later, that they did. They came out again only because I had called them to ask them if they would. It wasn't because they hadn't wanted to, but the sheriff's department had not contacted them with a need for it, and since we were given their number months earlier by the sheriff's office, we decided to go ahead and contact them ourselves. Of course, they would only come out if law enforcement was on board too.

Over the next few months, we continued our search at that property on our own even though we knew that we eventually wanted to get a community search set up.

Every time we would go out to search, our vehicles would get all scratched up from the tree branches on the side of the narrow road. Worrying about our vehicles getting scratched up was the least of our worries though.

Even when the weather got cooler, we continued to make plans to go out searching.

It seemed that every time we made plans though, the weather changed and prevented us from going.

Kristie and I began to feel like the weather was not a deterrent at all because we knew that God never made mistakes.

We started to think that maybe the bad weather was just what we needed until the time was right.

One time on Thanksgiving Day, Kristie, Bobby, Darvis, and I went out again to search. Snow had fallen the previous week so we knew that up in that elevation, the roads would be covered in snow.

How we made it out there driving in the snow is beyond me. We slipped constantly. Trees had fallen in the road and Bobby and Darvis had to lift them up and move them out of the way.

Eventually we got stuck in the snow, but, fortunately, it was close to a nearby home, and we were able to borrow a couple of shovels from them and dig ourselves out.

Within the next week, Darvis and I had gone out again and new trees had fallen, but this time Darvis came prepared. He brought his chainsaw.

The reason that we never went to the media to begin with or had another search going earlier is because we were told constantly by the Tuolumne County Sheriff's Department, and so believed it, that they already knew who most likely was behind Darvie's disappearance, and they were just waiting until someone would come forward and tell it all to them. They felt like it was going to happen soon, so if we would just be patient and wait, it was only a matter of time, and we would have our answers.

So many tips kept coming through the sheriff's office, and it always seemed like we were just about to get our answers. We were told someone new was always being talked to.

Time just went on and on…

From the very beginning, Kristie and I started having dreams where all we were doing in our dreams was searching.

Always searching for Darvie…

Searching for Darvie consumed our dreams nightly

Even now after many years, while I was out searching again, and I had a lot of things on my mind with the new information that I was given, I found my dreams again, starting to be consumed with thoughts of searching.

Darvis and I started taking anybody who seemed interested in checking out some other mines in the area. There were many other mines on the drive out to that property. However, every time a mine was checked, we were told that nothing was found.

Even though Darvie had fallen in a mine a couple of years earlier, and that all this property we were exploring was around mines, did not mean that Darvie had been in these mines.

We live in an area that is filled with mines, but we just didn't know if someone had hurt Darvie and then put him in one so we just wanted them checked out.

There are so many mines in the area, and we were so frustrated because we had to rely on others to tell us where all the abandoned mines were located.

We didn't necessarily trust everyone that went in the mines for us, but we felt like we had no other choice since these people were used to going in mines and were familiar with these particular ones. They didn't seem to mind going in them. In fact, they seemed to *enjoy* going in them.

Darvie always drank Pepsi, and it seemed so many mines that we checked out had a Pepsi can just lying around on the outside. I have wondered at times if someone planted the Pepsi cans there to confuse us and to keep us looking in the wrong area.

Many of the mines have garbage all around them, but most of the Pepsi cans have appeared newer and stood out all by themselves, without any other garbage around.

We also started hearing from more people. I was always getting more tips. I saw people all around town, who gave me ideas of new places to check out. They would always tell me '*what they had heard*'.

The thing that I always have said and that I will always continue to say to people when I talk to them about trying to find my son is, "Please call me *if* you hear *anything* because you don't know what I know, and you may just be giving me the *missing key* that I have been waiting for".

We started getting people who had contacted friends of theirs who claimed to be psychics and wanted to give us the information that they had received.

We listened to some of them, but as Christians we just did not want any part of that. We knew that the one who we believed in and put our whole trust in knew exactly what had happened, and where Darvie was. As frustrating as it was, we knew in his perfect timing if and when he wanted us to know, we would.

One time without us even knowing it, the sheriff's department went out on a tip from a supposed psychic and had to get all dirty and wet as they searched the creek. Though we do not believe we need to consult psychics we still very much appreciate the law enforcement doing that as they were still searching in an important area that needed to be searched.

Darvis and I continued going out to the property where Darvie's clothes and boots were found. It seemed like only a few days would go by, and we were out there again.

I just knew our son was out there. But where was he?

Both of us would go with anticipation of finding something, only to become discouraged as soon as we got out there. Since the area was so vast, we had to ask ourselves, "Where do we look?" or "Where do we even start?"

Every time we would get ready to leave the property, I was always the one that kept saying that I wanted to come back out again. Darvis and Kristie were always saying that they didn't want to come back, because of how discouraging it was, once we all got out there again.

Darvis kept trying to explain to me how someone would never know, if they had already checked a place out or not. There was too much land without really knowing where exactly to search. He said that it wasn't going to be as easy as I kept thinking it would be.

We all knew though that we just had to find someone to tell us where Darvie was. We could be searching the land for many years to come, with no results if we didn't.

We kept listening to the Tuolumne County Sheriff's Department telling us that the truth was surely *just around the corner.*

Truth is what we have always needed. We never knew while we were searching what really was the truth so we always felt discouraged while we searched.

As days became weeks, Darvis and I continued to go out to the property. We always wore our flannel jackets and heavy boots.

There was poison oak everywhere and for some reason, Darvis and I never really got it.

There was a couple of times though, that we would find small ticks on our body or clothes.

Darvis is susceptible to the MRSA (methicillin resistant staphylococcus aureus) infection, and one time I thought that he was going to break out with the infection again, because after I had taken a tick off of him, his skin had started to turn red and the redness had started to spread within a short time, but I believe because we prayed, the redness was gone by morning.

Everywhere we turned, there were piles of things and sunken areas. The terrain was filled with trees, fallen trees, bushes, and blackberry bushes. Poison oak and Manzanita bushes were everywhere.

Even the HRD team said the last time they came out to help us, that "They had never seen such consistent brush."

We never went down to the water's edge though.

Darvis and I always continued our search close to where Darvie's clothes were found and the embankment below the trailers. We kept always trying to find the *missing link* there.

There were also two small ammunition bunkers that had been built into the mountain on each side of one of the mines, close to where Darvie's clothes had been found. They were both locked, and we were very curious to see what was in them.

Sometimes Darvis would drive on the road, and I would walk slowly looking down the embankments. I was hoping to find anything that looked out of place. It was mainly thick terrain that I would see. If I suddenly found a clearing, I would quickly run down the bank and look around.

Darvis would wait for me as his legs just couldn't take the hike. However, he would have came down in a second, if needed.

Again, how my heart yearned to find my son.

7

During one time searching, Darvis and I came out alone with two shovels and a pick. We got separated from each other for awhile, and since I had one of the shovels and the pick that I insisted on bringing, my load was very heavy. We started at the top of the mountain and climbed down. I kept thinking about mountain lions and didn't know how I would ever be able to get away with such heavy boots on, if I ever did see one.

For me to even worry about seeing an animal, let alone a mountain lion was strange, because for some reason way out there in the wilderness we had never seen deer, foxes, squirrels, etc. In fact, we had never seen a living animal up there, nor ever been aware of any birds chirping out there.

No animal droppings of any kind have ever been found except one time I saw bear droppings. It kind of freaked me out when I came upon it. I was climbing up a real steep embankment at the time and had no way out, but up. At that particular time, I was quickly trying to climb up the mountain, and I slipped and hit my head hard against a sharp edge of a pointed branch. Luckily my forehead was the only thing that took the hit.

Since the Tuolumne County Sheriff's Office had never questioned Henry who lived above the property about anything, Darvis and I decided to go and have a talk with him.

I asked him if he had heard anything outside, around the time that Darvie was supposed to have been up there in the area. He said that he hadn't, but, at times, he said he had heard people banging on equipment down below.

He said Chuck and him had a deal between the two of them that when Chuck was down at his property he would ring a big bell down below, and then Henry was to ring the bell up at his house to let Chuck know that he had heard him and knew that he was the one down there on his property.

One time when we knew that Henry was home while we were down below on the property, we rang the bell but nothing happened. Even Bobby, while he was up on Henry's property had yelled down to us from up above to see if we could hear him but we could not.

Henry had a dog named Max that was a Labrador mix. He was a beautiful dog.

At the very beginning, as we searched below Henry's house, Max would show up. He never let us get too close to him but would run about, all around us. He was real skittish. He never barked either.

One time, shortly after our visit with Henry, Darvis and I came back out to the property to search for Darvie. I wanted to go to Henry's house first to ask him some more questions.

This ended up being an intervention made by God.

As soon as we knocked on the door we heard someone yelling. They were calling out for help.

The front door was locked. However, the back door was not.

We followed the cry for help as we ran up the stairs. We found Henry lying on his bed. He said he had been stuck in bed for at least a week. He had gone without food and water because he had not been able to get up. Though I did not know if Henry could be trusted or not. Darvis and I would have helped this old man out regardless.

Henry's dog Max had been stuck in the house the whole time too but he had food and water downstairs in big pots that were not quite empty. Dog feces were everywhere. I tried helping out by cleaning up a little.

Darvis called 911 but he had to meet the paramedics down the road a ways to bring them in his truck. The road going up to Henry's property was just too rough for an ambulance vehicle to drive up on. It was also too hard to explain to anyone exactly where to go, to find Henry's place.

While Darvis was gone to wait for the ambulance, I took the opportunity to ask Henry some questions. We had recently been given some new information regarding Chuck's behavior during the time Darvie went missing. I wanted to know what Henry had heard from Chuck, if anything.

It wasn't long until Darvis got back with the paramedics.

Since Max was such a hyper dog, he was still kind of skittish in his own home around strangers. I was able to grab a hold of Max's collar to keep him from running around everywhere.

The paramedics put Henry on a stretcher, took him down, and put him in the back of the bed of our truck.

Darvis and I knew that we could not leave Max behind so we made plans to take the dog with us while Henry went to the hospital.

We got Max inside the truck and headed down with everyone else in the back of our truck, to where the ambulance was parked.

It didn't take long for Max to know that he could trust us.

Henry ended up having severe gout so he had to stay in the hospital. We ended up keeping Max for a few weeks until Henry got out.

In the past, Henry had told us that he took Max with him only once a week when he would go into town. Max was used to being out in the boonies with hardly any sounds around. He wasn't really around other people and no other dogs at all. However, Max got along with our two little dachshunds.

While Max was with us, he never barked.

I started thinking that he was deaf. But one time after Max had been with us a couple of weeks, when our neighbor came inside our house he let out just a little whimper bark, which surprised us all.

While Max was with us, we got rid of all the big ticks that he had on him from being out in the wilderness so much up at Henry's house.

Max jumped on our bed constantly. He expected to sleep on the bed with us at night. He licked Darvis in the face in the morning when he wanted to go outside and eventually he won our heart.

The only problem that we seemed to have with Max, was for some reason, when we would gently go to grab his collar around his neck to lead him somewhere, at times he would put his mouth on our hand like telling us that he didn't want us to do that.

When Henry got out of the hospital, his son Jerry who lived in another state, came and picked up Max. We were sad to see Max go. I mentioned to Jerry that if his dad ever gave Max away for any reason, we would take him.

It wasn't long after that when Henry's son called Darvis and said that his dad told him that Max had been bringing bones home.

With sadness and yet a little hope, I had to filter that information through my heart somehow.

When we got up there to Henry's house, I was determined to find out what Max had brought home.

But Henry never could really remember where he threw the bones that Max had brought home.

I was so frustrated that we never could get much information out of the old man.

We went over to an area on his property that Henry had said where some of his other dogs that had died were buried. Henry figured that was where Max had been digging up the bones. However, the dirt did not look like it had been recently disturbed at all.

As soon as I started digging with a shovel and realized how hard the ground was and that Henry had said it was just where he had buried his animals at, I felt defeated and quickly stopped.

We went back up to the house and went inside for just a few minutes. I was just hoping that Henry would tell us something new on his own that we needed to know, but he never did.

Max was a little skittish around us again at first but after we sat down, he warmed up to us, and we could tell that he finally remembered us.

Max, was rambunctious, and he started jumping on top of Henry's feet so Henry kept picking up a heavy curtain rod and threatening Max with it from time to time. As soon as we saw that, we kept calling Max over to us.

The story with Max does end well.

Henry's son eventually called Darvis again. He said his dad was back in the hospital and he did not know how long he would be in there, but he thought it might be for good. Jerry asked us if we would take Max permanently as our own.

The answer was, yes!

Unfortunately, when Max came back a year later, he was a different dog.

We noticed that Henry had put a choke chain on Max since the last time we were up there. It seemed to us that someone must have been yanking on his choke chain, trying to get him to mind them, because the first day we got Max back, he bit Darvis on one of his hands when his collar was gently grabbed to lead him somewhere. We had a couple more situations with Max that same day that made Darvis and I wonder if we should have taken Max back now that things were so different.

Max had also been penned up for awhile in a small backyard at Henry's, instead of being able to roam around in the mountains like he had been used to doing.

He was now territorial and had a bark that sounded very ferocious.

But we held out and the next day Darvis closed in our backyard and we decided that we would give him a chance.

It took Darvis a week to cut the choke chain off and put a new collar on him.

We had to earn Max's trust again.

We got Max neutered a couple of months later in hopes that it would calm him down and it did.

He is a different dog now.

He is still territorial with other dogs and somewhat with people coming in our house if he is inside but if someone is in the house when he comes in, he is okay.

Max has become part of our family, and now almost three years later, we adore him.

The way Darvis and I feel, we have some kind of a kinship with Max.

Since Max was up there on Henry's property, in the vicinity when Darvie possibly ended up there and then when something may have happened to him...

If Max could only speak...

8

It is so ironic that we ended up with our dog Max because if Darvie had not gone missing, and, if we had never been led up to that property from the very beginning, we would not have Max today.

So even though I appreciated that Henry gave us Max, I have never completely trusted Henry when it came to anything to do with Darvie. I do not know if Henry knows something that he's just not telling us; however I am still grateful that God may have used us to save Henry's life.

We were told by one of Henry's relative's, "I'm not so sure Darvie didn't end up at Henry's house. Darvie could have been coming up there in the dark possibly running for help from someone, and Henry could have got scared and not knowing him, shot him."

Then they said, "Or Chuck could have done something to him, and then Henry helped Chuck out."

The things that people have told us…

At another time, the same relative brought up another story to Darvis that broke my heart even more, and even today, I have a hard time even thinking about it.

I had to actually call them up and say, "I'm not saying that we don't believe you, but *please* make sure what you tell us is *really* the complete truth because these things being said to us are too painful to hear. We do want to hear things *if* these things really happened but we don't want to hear anything unless it is a "for sure" thing".

So many people get carried away with their words sometimes. Although they think they could possibly be helping us, they don't think far enough ahead to realize how they are hurting us with the words that they say especially if it is not true or just an assumption.

Hearing assumptions and rumors such as these that so many people have told me is so hard for my heart to bear at times. I cannot wait until one day this nightmare is all over, as best as it can be.

Unfortunately, Henry has gotten more forgetful in his old age.

I feel it will not be possible to get any help from him at all.

Remember the day that I had talked with Henry when we were waiting for the paramedics to come get him to take him to the hospital?

I had asked Henry then what he had heard from Chuck, if anything about our son.

He confirmed having, heard the same information that we had heard before, but he described it differently, like in a nonchalant way, like it wasn't our son that he was talking about.

It made me so sad…

What we weren't told, was even worse than what we had been told originally.

What Chuck did, is so horrible, it is almost too hard for me, to even write it down on paper.

If one day we find out that Chuck is guilty *only* of these horrible actions, the world still needs to know what he did.

The story must be told…

9

These next accounts of what happened during the time Darvie went missing is everything that I can remember to the best of my ability, and I have wrote it down as accurately as I can remember after I was told about it.

Keep in mind, Monday October 18, 2010 was the last time we saw or talked to Darvie.

Sunday, October 17 or Monday, October 18, 2010

Chuck the landowner called the sheriff's office to tell them that there had been people on his property.

What is weird to me is that supposedly Mark had already been going on the property for a few months at this point, so why make the call then?

Chuck had even painted all those words on his gate and bulldozer months earlier.

Early in the morning of October 19, 2010, my family and I have always felt is the day when something happened to Darvie.

Tuesday, October 19 or Wednesday, October 20, 2010

Chuck called the sheriff's office again but this time it was to ask them what "his rights" were as far as people being on his property.

The sheriff's department told him that he couldn't shoot anyone, but that he could arm himself for protection.

I have always wondered, had something already happened? Was that the reason why he called to ask what "his rights" were?

So you could say that Chuck made two important phone calls to the sheriff's office.

Totally understandable if people were hanging out on your property, and you wanted to find out what your rights were just in case you met up with somebody on your property.

But Chuck never called the sheriff's office again after he made those two phone calls nor had he made calls previously.

It was the Tuolumne County Sheriff's Office, who ended up calling Chuck, to ask him to come in over a week and a half later, when they realized he was the landowner of the place where Darvie's clothes and boots were found.

What Chuck did after he made those two phone calls, I will never be able to understand.

10

Sometime in the next several days, between Wednesday, October 20, and Monday, October 25, if it hadn't happened already, Chuck supposedly just *came upon* Darvie's clothes laying out on his property.

Chuck said he found Darvie's work boots over on top of a boat by one of the mines.

But what he did next just doesn't make any sense.

Chuck took out a gun and decided to shoot Darvie's boots up, and, since he didn't want to shoot out in the open sky with the boots on the boat, he put the boots down on the ground and shot them up there.

Chuck then went back over to where the jeans were supposedly laying and shot them up too.

Remember the tear in Darvie's jeans that we had seen when we had found them, when I had thought that Darvie may have torn them on something like barbed wire? We would have never thought that a gunshot had done that. We also never noticed at the time when Darvie's boots were found that any gunshot holes had been put in them either. Our minds were so horrified at finding his personal belongings in such a way, we blocked out the bullet holes we were seeing.

When I found out about Chuck shooting up Darvie's clothes and boots, I could hardly take in that information without feeling so broken inside.

We were so shocked!

What would have made a man go to such an extreme such as that?

Chuck then said that he took out his *new* cell phone that he had *just* purchased and took pictures of all the items that he had found.

But what we hadn't been told by the sheriff's office until about a week later was that Darvie's dentures had also been found and that Chuck had shot them up too.

If that isn't enough to shock you, Chuck then walked the long way back up the dirt road, all the way to the gate at the top of the driveway carrying Darvie's boots tied together with one of Darvie's shot up denture plates in one of the boots and hung them on the gate.

None of us at the time that Darvie's boots were found even looked inside them. Detective Bob had taken them and had possession of them.

Darvis was the one who had been given this new information. He had intentionally not mentioned it to me yet.

But a few days later while Darvis, Bobby, Kristie, and I were out searching, I accidentally overheard some talk that Darvie's dentures had been found and shot up also by Chuck. Darvie always wore his dentures in public so I had to shove that information to the back of my mind immediately because it was way too painful for me to take in at the time.

It was not until we got home that I actually got Darvis to confirm that what I dreaded acknowledging was in fact the truth.

After I was able to let it sink in a little, it was then in my own home with my heart completely broken I finally was able to release my tears.

Horrified, I kept thinking, "My son's *teeth* were shot up???!!!

What kind of person *could* or *would* actually do something like that?

Why would Chuck not think that the things that he found on his property might just belong to someone who was homeless, just passing through, and meant no harm?

Surely, *that* would have been the time for him to call the Tuolumne County Sheriff's Office back again when he actually found someone's clothes and boots and especially now their *teeth?*

But remember Chuck never called the sheriff's office after he found Darvie's things, shot them up, took pictures of everything, and went back home.

Even after we filed the Missing Person's Report, and it was put in our local newspaper; Chuck never came forward.

It was after Chuck was contacted by the Tuolumne County Sheriff's Department that he ended up telling them about his new cell phone, and how he had taken pictures of everything. Chuck then offered his new cell phone for law enforcement to take if they needed to so that they could see the pictures. The sheriff's office took it from Chuck but gave it back to him a short time later.

Sound convenient?

It wasn't until weeks later, when I was questioning Detective Bob about why Chuck's phone was given back to him, that I was told that the pictures were blurry and they could hardly make out what the pictures were anyway.

That frustrated me so much because I wanted to see for myself what exactly those pictures looked like.

Chuck even gave the key to his gate to the sheriff's office so that they would have it if they needed it. He seemed more than willing to cooperate with them.

This is when we found out from Detective Bob that Chuck had written all those words on his gate and bulldozer a few months earlier, way before Darvie was even back in town.

Gloria also confirmed that when Mark and Debby had taken her up to the property, she had seen the words painted on the gate and bulldozer then.

If Chuck had written those words on the gate and bulldozer more recently, to me that would have made more sense.

But who knows what future intentions Chuck may have had when he wrote those words, if anyone ever came on his property *again* and he was to find them on it?

After Darvie's clothes and boots had been found but *before* we knew any information about Chuck shooting anything up, Darvis and I decided to stop by Chuck's house.

We had been told that Chuck owned the property, and we just wanted to see what he knew.

Remember, ironically Chuck lived below us on the same road.

Chuck came out of his house as soon as we drove up. When we got out of our vehicle, Darvis asked him if he would go out with us to the property and show us around.

He said that the sheriff's office had told him that they did not want him up there.

We found out later from the detective that the sheriff's office had never told Chuck that.

We then asked Chuck if he could just at least tell us what he knew.

He agreed to, but, first, he did something I found to be strange.

He went inside his house and came back with some licorice.

He chewed on the licorice the whole time as he began to tell a story that was told to us detail by detail..., like it was well rehearsed.

At that time, we never thought of Chuck as a person of interest. We just knew that it was his property, and our son's things had been found there. We also knew that Darvie did not know Chuck.

One of the things that he told us was that he had went down to the trailers on his property, looked inside, and had seen a VW axle on the floor next to a cold half-drank can of beer.

Darvie wasn't a beer drinker, and we found out later that it was the kind of beer that Mark drank.

Chuck said that it made him realize that someone was *arming themselves* with this *weapon* so he took the VW axle with him and put it in the back of his truck.

As far as we know, Chuck kept the axle in the back of his truck for quite awhile. The Tuolumne County Sheriff's Office, even though they looked at it, never confiscated that item either.

Darvis has always said that this statement Chuck made didn't make any sense because there were weapons all over the place on that property if you just look around.

At one point, Chuck went back inside his house while we were talking to him and brought out a surveillance camera that he said he was going to be putting up at the property because people were always going up there and stealing things.

When we felt like Chuck had told us all that he was going to tell us, we got in our vehicle and went back home.

After we left Chuck's house, Darvis and I talked about how we felt. We both agreed that we didn't really feel like we had received any new information from Chuck than what had already been told to us.

Darvis said that he couldn't understand though, why Chuck didn't seem to have any compassion?

Especially after we found out later on that Chuck had shot up our son's possessions, besides showing no compassion, we even wondered why Chuck hadn't felt the need to apologize to us for at least something. Even though we did not know what Chuck had done, he knew.

Darvis always felt like if he had been in the same situation himself, he would have done things a lot differently. He said if he knew what he had done to neighbors' loved one's possessions and then they had came by to talk to him to try to get some answers, he would at least have apologized. Apologized for doing *something* that he did not realize at the time he was doing to *their* loved one's belongings?

Detective Bob did finally go over and talk with Chuck at his home one time and asked Chuck to take him up to the property to look around.

We had been urging Detective Bob to get Chuck to open up the two small ammunition bunkers. The detective told us that after they had went up there, Chuck *on his own* offered to unlock them and open them up. They were very small and the detective said that nothing was found inside.

The detective said that Chuck even agreed to take a lie detector test if they needed him to.

My family and I eventually started thinking that Chuck should be seriously looked at as a person of interest by the sheriff's office.

But every time we brought it up, the Tuolumne County Sheriff's Office always acted like they did not think Chuck was the one who had done *anything* to Darvie.

Instead the sheriff's office was trying to get a hold of Mark to bring him in since he was still running from the law on a prior incident, but they couldn't find him.

Every time they got sight of Mark, he was able to run off again and escape.

11

One evening a little over a week after Darvie went missing, Darvis got a call telling us where Mark was hiding out. We called the Tuolumne County Sheriff's Office and they quickly went and caught him before he could escape again.

Supposedly when law enforcement entered the house where Mark was at, he had covered himself with a sleeping bag. When they pulled it off of him, he said to them, "I'm tired of running."

Now with Mark in our local county jail, I felt prompted by the Lord to write him a letter.

At the beginning of my letter, I explained to Mark how for years I had been acquainted with some of his family.

I asked him to picture in his mind someone whom he cared about and loved a whole lot. When he got that person in his mind, I told him that was how much I loved my son.

I told him he knew as well as I knew that he was not just out walking with my son on a road, and Darvie just *disappeared*.

I told him I had heard that he had a small child, and that I did not know if he was even in contact with that child, but that he needed to make his child proud of him and do the *right* thing.

I told him we will all have to answer to God someday, and it is better to do it now than later.

I asked him to *please* tell me where my son was.

I never got a response from him.

However, I do know that he received my letter because he had mentioned it to Detective Bob.

I was so bummed. I had hoped Mark would have had compassion while reading my letter and decide to come forward with the truth, no matter what it was.

I was hoping, besides being tired of running, that Mark would have also been tired of not telling the whole truth.

Yet every time Mark was questioned by the sheriff's office, he kept changing his story.

One story I heard he told was the same one that we had heard from Gloria. The one about where Mark said Darvie had been down on the property cutting brush below, and that he was up messing around with a rock crusher when they heard someone coming in their vehicle playing loud music. Then all of a sudden it became completely silent.

He said he told Darvie to be quiet, but Darvie kept making sounds in the brush.

Mark said he went and hid under the boat over by the entrance of one of the mines, and he saw the landowner walking by with a Mossberg Shotgun.

He said when he and Darvie thought they heard the landowner leave in his vehicle, they started heading back to Mark's truck. Mark said they had to go up a trail but that he had told Darvie to walk about thirty feet behind him the whole time.

There is rarely any cell service out there, but he said Darvie was fiddling on his phone the whole time as they were heading up the trail.

To think that Darvie was really messing with his phone because he might have been trying frantically to call us to help him in an emergency, just breaks my heart so deeply.

When Darvie had fallen in the mine a couple of years earlier, all he kept saying is that he wanted me.

How I wish I could have been there for my son.

Mark said Darvie had dropped the only flashlight they had while walking up the trail. Mark said it was a small flashlight that belonged to him.

A small flashlight was actually found on the trail, but Gloria told me that it was her flashlight that Mark had borrowed from her in the past and had never given it back to her.

Mark said when he turned around once he got up to the road, Darvie had disappeared. He said he drove around back and forth on the road for awhile to see if he could find Darvie.

Yet at another time, Mark said that once he made it up the trail and realized Darvie wasn't behind him, he had sat in his truck, covered up with the seat cover and slept there for a couple of hours and waited, but Darvie never came back. Mark said that he had his truck parked on a slant because he had to roll it to get it to start.

Another thing Mark said was when he kept telling Darvie to be quiet and Darvie was still being so loud that Mark finally said to him, "Shut up or I'm going to kill you!"

The last story Mark gave to the Tuolumne County Sheriff's Office was supposedly that Darvie and him had made it up to his truck but that they were arguing. Some think this statement proves that Mark was the one behind Darvie's disappearance.

To me, even with Mark saying those words doesn't make it the truth.

After Mark had been arrested, we found out where Mark's truck was. Bobby and Kristie happened to be with us at the time, so we all went and checked it out.

The seat cover in the vehicle didn't look like it had ever been off at all, and, as my husband suspected, it had an automatic transmission, which you cannot roll to start.

His truck was a beat-up old truck that had no doors on it and no hood. The headlights were mounted up above the roof of the vehicle.

It was a sight to see for sure.

This vehicle could never have been driven around town. It would have only been able to be driven out on the back roads up where it was found. Out in the boonies would have been the only place to drive it without getting stopped by law enforcement.

In the back of Mark's truck was a six-by-six pressure-treated timber block of wood, a plastic bin, a plastic crate bin, clothes were strewn here and there, a cable, an electrical wire, a small propane tank, a tarp and a bunch of miscellaneous pieces of junk.

Mark's truck was looked over by the Tuolumne County Sheriff's Office, and it ended up being disengaged so it couldn't run, but, unfortunately, it was never impounded to have it checked out more thoroughly.

Not long afterwards, someone took it away and supposedly parted it out.

It has never been seen again.

I actually called the person whom Mark had gotten it from, but the man told me that he had not seen it anywhere. I even checked with the local wrecking yard and some local towing companies and showed them a picture of it, but they had no remembrance of ever seeing it before.

Finally Detective Bob went to talk to Debby. He was a believer in the Lord like we are, and so he tried to explain to her that we would all have to answer to God someday and that if she knew anything at all that she had not told him before, now was the time to tell him.

She continued to say that she knew nothing.

In the meantime Darvie's estranged wife Paula called Darvis and asked him what was going on. He told her it was none of her business because he felt like she was the reason this had even happened to Darvie.

Darvis and I both felt that there was a good chance that some of her acquaintances may have been responsible for Darvie's disappearance somehow. There was a connection between Mark and some of them.

We figured Paula had ulterior motives when she called anyway.

Sure enough it didn't take long before we began hearing that Darvie's estranged wife was calling around the tow yards, inquiring about where his car was.

And speaking of where his car was, it was still parked in our driveway.

On one particular day, *only* two weeks after Darvie had went missing, Kristie was at our house, and Darvis told me that he was going to go and clean out Darvie's car.

I had to leave to go uptown so I left right away.

Kristie said that Darvis started bringing in all kinds of things with tears down his face and giving it to her to bring inside the house. She said at one point she was wondering why he was bringing all the stuff in.

The car was emptied of everything.

Darvis and Kristie said only about a half hour after that, they were sitting in the living room with the back door open when they heard something. They looked out and were shocked to see law enforcement near Darvie's car. They saw someone rush over to Darvie's car and get in, and the officer told the person to wait a minute.

Darvis and Kristie realized that the person getting in Darvie's car was his estranged wife Paula.

The officer told Darvis and Kristie that legally they had to release the vehicle to her.

Darvis had to move a vehicle blocking Darvie's car in so his car could be removed.

With a smirk on her face, Paula drove away.

She didn't even pay the tow bill.

When Darvis called me to tell me what had just happened, all I could do was be in awe of what God had just done for us.

It was horrible that the vehicle was taken from us in the way that it was, and it was frustrating that the sheriff's office had not impounded the car. But I was amazed that God had given Darvis the notion to clean out Darvie's car, and that he had cleaned it out right away.

To get every single thing out of it because within one half hour unbeknownst to us, Darvie's car was going to leave us forever was amazing to me.

Wow!

What we were able to get out of the car was priceless beyond the value of what any vehicle could be.

We found out that Paula while she was in town went and visited Mark while he was at the county jail. We had heard that law enforcement had listened to their conversation, but they were not able to pick up on anything that had been said that could help us.

I felt that Paula and Debby had to have been in contact with each other for Debby to let Paula use her visiting time with Mark at the jail.

Gloria had even told me that Paula had called over to Debby's when she happened to be over there before Gloria and Debby's friendship completely dissolved.

Paula may have began to feel guilty because we heard that after she had taken Darvie's car, (that was maybe worth up to a $1,500 value), she had began to tell people in our town that she was going to sell the vehicle to help toward the reward that we had offered to the community at the time to help us find him.

She never did.

Paula has never done anything to help us. Paula has never even offered to help search for Darvie either.

I also heard from an acquaintance that Darvie wasn't even missing two weeks, and Paula decided to get baptized at a church.

I wondered why she wouldn't wait to do that until her estranged husband was found?

After Darvie's car was taken, along with the gratitude that we felt seeing God's hand in the situation, came a lot of new questions for us.

Even though we knew in our hearts that something had happened to Darvie but that we just didn't know what yet, I kept thinking, *If her estranged husband had only been missing for a couple of weeks and could maybe resurface eventually and come back to get the vehicle that was actually his, why would she come all the way down from Oregon to get his car, to drive it all the way back up there, in case he was found soon?*

Unless…Unless maybe she knew something we didn't know?

That he was never coming back?

12

Our minds and bodies were so worn out from all the things that we had been enduring. However, we continued putting up more missing person flyers.

At this time, we increased the reward to $15,000 to anyone who could lead us to the arrest and conviction of whomever was responsible for Darvie's disappearance.

On one particular day, we were in the neighborhood where Darvie's car was found. We happened to be tacking a flyer on a tree, and Debby came driving around the corner.

As she was driving by, Darvis said to her, "You're going to get caught".

She then stopped her vehicle and started saying that she and Darvie were friends and that she was trying to get Mark to tell her anything but that he never did.

I looked at her and told her that she was not my son's friend. I told her that only her acquaintances in Oregon and her were the only ones that would want to get revenge.

Darvis told her that we would never stop looking for our son.

With so much frustration built up inside him, Darvis kicked Debby's beat-up old truck a couple of times.

She said she was going to go call the cops.

With that, she drove away.

We were going to go talk with Detective Bob when we were done putting up the flyers anyway, so we figured that we would tell him all about what had just happened then.

Debby did call Detective Bob and talk with him about it. We heard that she was told by someone, "Their son's car was found in your driveway, you sell drugs to people, and now their son has been *missing* for seven weeks! You should be happy that's the only thing they did to you".

I do know the frustration of seeing Debby and knowing that she *knew* where our son was and acting like she could care less just got the best of my husband for a moment.

Lie detector tests were now being set up as Mark who was still in our county jail and Debby both agreed to take one.

We were very anxious to see what the results were going to be.

Mark and Debby each took a lie detector test down at the sheriff's office within a matter of days.

We heard later through a reliable source that Mark had failed his test completely, and it was on the most important issues that Debby failed.

At least now as we had already suspected, they were definitely involved somehow.

Eventually though, another guy's name, Louie, was brought up.

A relative of mine called to tell me that they had seen Louie, and Louie told them that he had been with Darvie just a few days before he went missing.

He said that Darvie and him had been at Debby's house together but had left separately. Soon afterward Louie said that he himself started getting sick. He felt that he might have been poisoned with some drugs, and so he thought that maybe Darvie might have gotten poisoned also.

We contacted the sheriff's office to give Detective Bob this new information. He told us that he too had started to hear Louie's name being brought up through the people that he was interviewing.

Shortly after we heard this, Darvis and I were called over to an acquaintance's house, and a woman, Linda was there. She told us that she had heard from a guy named Tim about what had actually happened. The scenario included Mark, a guy named Louie, a girl named Maria, and Darvie. Ironically Mark's truck had been found parked at Maria's house.

The scenario that she described brought tears to my eyes.

What had this evil world come to?

Linda acted so sure that the story that she was telling us was the truth.

Darvis and I then left, contacted Detective Bob, who made plans to look up this guy Tim and go talk with him.

Within a few days of hearing this, I got a call from a relative of Louie's, named Shirley who told me that Louie was in the hospital and was getting ready to have a very serious surgery. A surgery that was needed because supposedly Louie would have died without it.

One of his other family members that I was barely acquainted with later told me while Louie was medicated and before he went in to have his surgery Louie was saying, "They are going to hurt me, like they hurt Darvie".

Whether that was told to me to make Louie not look like a suspect I do not know.

But at this point, we did not look at Louie like he was a person of interest yet.

We just felt like Louie may have the missing answers that we so desperately needed for all the questions that we had.

Darvis and I had wanted to go talk to Louie while he was in the hospital, so a couple of days after Louie had his surgery, we were told by a relative of his that Louie had told them we could come by and talk with him if we wanted to.

Everything was happening at once, and it seemed that soon we would have some answers.

In the meantime, Detective Bob went to the hospital and spent a couple of hours talking with Louie.

Louie's story began to change from what I had originally been told.

He now started saying that Mark was with him at a mine site when he started getting sick after he shot up some drugs that Mark had given him. It was at the same property where Darvie's clothes had been found. However, he said nothing about him being with Darvie at all.

In fact, Louie told Detective Bob that he didn't know who Darvie was and had maybe only heard his name years ago from when he used to be in school. It seemed like not much came from their conversation.

Darvis and I made plans to go see Louie.

When we got to the hospital, Louie basically told us the same story that he had told the detective about thinking that Mark had tried to poison him so that maybe Mark had tried to poison our son too.

When we questioned him about where he was on the property, Louie described a mine on Chuck's property that he had explored inside with Mark. He said that there was a big room inside toward the back of the mine that you could go and stand in. Louie said it was about the size of his small hospital room.

What he made us believe is that it was the lower mine on that property where the water continuously flowed out of.

Louie had said that he had noticed something in the needle before he shot it up in his arm.

He said that he didn't really know what it was, but he shot it into his arm anyway.

All of a sudden, he said, he began to feel like something was wrong and it was then that he began to think that Mark had poisoned him.

He said he then ran to get away, but, in the condition he was in, it took him about an hour and a half to get out of the area and make it to Maria's house.

Louie had no problem accusing Mark of any wrongdoings as Mark was now back in prison doing more time for a parole violation.

Louie told us there was a crazy landowner around there.

When I questioned him further about the landowner, he said that Mark had told him that the landowner had shot at him before.

While we were there talking with Louie, Darvis stepped out of the room for a moment, and I asked Louie about the scenario that we had heard from Linda that had happened at Maria's house.

All he said without looking at me was, "Oh, that is what they said, but I don't remember that."

For some reason maybe because my mind was filled with so many questions, I never really thought to expand on it. It was a scenario that I did not want to believe anyway.

Since Louie acted like he did not know Darvie, I completely forgot about the phone call I had originally received where Louie had said he had been with Darvie just days before he went missing.

It was really from that original phone call, why Darvis and I had wanted to go see Louie to begin with.

I had forgotten to mention anything about it at all even though it was so important to me to have questioned him about it.

I couldn't even understand why I had done that.

Later on I figured for some reason it just must have been God's will that I had forgotten about it at the time.

But before we left, even though I had forgotten about the phone call that I had received, I looked Louie straight in the eye and asked him, "So you did not know Darvie?"

He said, "No."

Then I asked him, "And, you did not see Darvie in the seventeen days that he was here?"

Again, he answered, "No".

We walked outside with Louie, as he was saying that he needed a cigarette really badly. He told us that when he was released from the hospital he was going to move out of town.

He said that not many people knew that he was leaving.

I now wonder, what was the big secret?

I actually gave Louie a hug and Darvis shook his hand as we thanked him for talking to us.

Nothing out of the ordinary seemed apparent at the time.

I still did not think Louie was a person of interest even after talking with him.

I just thought that he might have been someone who could have given us some answers, but then after talking with Louie, I realized we hadn't gotten anything from him that I had hoped for.

Looking back now, there were so many things that I wished I would have said to Louie.

So many questions weren't answered.

I felt good about talking with Louie though, and how everything went during our visit but I was soon to find out that Darvis did not have a good feeling toward Louie at all.

After we left Louie at the hospital, I called the relative of mine and told them the things that we had discussed. I also mentioned that Louie had said that he didn't know Darvie. Immediately the person said, "He knows Darvie!"

A few days after that, someone else called me just to confirm that Louie had indeed known Darvie. They said that Louie had actually been at their home months earlier before Darvie went missing, and they had all been talking about Darvie.

Nothing was adding up now.

Detective Bob found out where the guy Tim was staying. He wanted to talk to Tim regarding the horrible scenario he had supposedly told Linda, who in turn told Darvis and I.

The detective arrived unannounced and was able to talk with Tim,

But all Tim did, the detective said, was deny everything and acted like he knew nothing.

Tim's girlfriend, Karen, was there when the detective talked to Tim. When Tim went back inside the house she quickly told the detective that he was pretty much on the right track with the scenario that he had mentioned regardless of what Tim had told him.

Karen was supposedly also a friend of Darvie's.

In fact, Darvie had contacted her a few times in the seventeen days that he was back in town. Darvie's phone records showed that they had been texting each other, but, according to Karen, they never met up.

She said that they always missed each other, wherever they both ended up at.

We have nothing that proves if they met up with each other or not.

Karen has been one that I have never trusted either, because in the beginning Karen's name had also come up. When we got her phone number, Darvis had called her, and she answered right away but the cell phone connection wasn't very good.

She said that she would call him right back. She never did. So Darvis had to call her again when we realized that she was not calling him back. This time an hour later they had a good connection. Karen acted like she knew nothing.

Eventually, Louie's name started being brought up often, by many of the people that we talked to.

When things didn't start to add up quite right, Darvis and I began to look at Louie as a person of interest instead of the victim he had tried to portray himself as. Even Detective Bob felt like Louie knew things that he was not telling.

Louie moved out of town as he said he was going to and so the communication with him and the detective wasn't very good.

When Detective Bob did eventually get a hold of him, he told Louie, "I think there is something that you need to tell me", and Louie said back to him, "Yeah…, I think there is".

When Darvis and I heard that, we were so encouraged that *finally* we were going to get the answers that we had waited so long to hear.

Detective Bob and Louie made plans for Louie to come take a lie detector test. Louie agreed to come back to town on a specific day to take it.

The detective got all the details worked out. A man from out of town was going to come in to give the test to Louie.

The day for the test to be taken had finally arrived. Louie had now returned back to our town.

Even though the detective knew where Louie was staying, he still left it up to Louie to bring himself in to take the test, which I did not understand.

The detective did not know though that once Louie got back into town, he would have a change of heart.

Louie never showed up to take the lie detector test.

It would be a long time before Louie would ever again, agree to take one.

13

We felt so let down when Louie didn't show up to take his lie detector test. We felt like our hands were tied.

We could only trust the Lord with what the future held. We knew he was our only hope.

In the very beginning, people would ask me from time to time if I thought Darvie might of just went away on purpose and needed time to be alone and did not want to be bothered by anyone for awhile? I would always tell them, "Absolutely not!"

Darvie was too connected to us to ever be able to do that. Emotionally he could never have done that.

Having people around him that he loved, his car, phone, money, etc. was all the things that had built Darvie's self-esteem. Darvie and I usually talked at least once a day.

For me, his absence has changed my days in such a drastic way.

So many tips came into the Tuolumne County Sheriff's Office. As the tips came in, I am pretty sure that most of them were checked out, but nothing ever *really* led us to anything.

The sheriff's office had people working behind the scenes at times, undercover so to speak, trying to find out whatever information that they could get.

I kept putting missing person flyers up around town on every bulletin board that I could find.

I even had flyers with Darvie's picture taped to each of my car's back passenger windows for about a year and a half.

Sometimes I would see one of the flyers gone that I had put out somewhere, and I would think that *just maybe* someone knew him and wanted the flyer for some reason.

At one location where we had put a flyer up, I saw just the corners left of the flyer. It was like someone had ripped it off, but, again, I tried to just believe that someone who knew him wanted to have the flyer.

Seeing the corners left, stuck with me quite awhile, and I eventually stopped at the location and took the taped corners down. I couldn't bear to drive by it and see it anymore.

As much as I have seen God's hand helping me in so many ways, I still cannot believe all the evil that I have seen throughout this whole ordeal.

One horrible thing that happened to me was on a Saturday morning in December 2010 when I was walking down the main street in our town looking through the stores as people all around were doing their Christmas shopping.

I had a teenage girl, who was living with us at the time, and a baby that I was taking care of with me, so I had a stroller that I was pushing along.

Every time I would walk by a store and see a good place to put a flyer, I would put one up. Even though I had a lot of flyers with me, it wasn't like I was putting them up *everywhere* around town though.

I came upon a pole in front of a store, and I began to tape a flyer on it.

As soon as I was done taping the flyer on the pole, an elderly man came right behind me and started tearing it down as he said to me, "You can't put these up all around town."

I turned to him and immediately began to tear up and I told him, "My son is missing."

He said, "It doesn't matter. This is not Berkeley, (Berkeley is a big liberal culture, very diverse, a city described as *eclectic*) where you can put them up at every street corner."

I said again to him with tears in my eyes, "But *my son* is *missing!*"

I just couldn't believe what was happening.

I asked him if he was a store owner.

I told him that I knew that the city workers would be *okay* with me putting them up.

He told me, "There are bulletin boards that you could put them up at."

I turned toward his wife, and she shook her head disgustedly at me and said, "As you put them up, we will take them down."

With that, they walked away.

I think I was in a state of shock from what they had just done to me.

The more I thought of it, I *had* noticed as we were putting the flyers up around town that some of the flyers did seem like they were gone from where I had put them up at earlier. I had just not given it much thought at the time.

We went into the store that we were right in front of and as soon as we entered I looked around hoping to see someone, anyone, who was in there that had just witnessed this *horrible* event that had just taken place outside, but no one seemed aware of anything.

My friend and I just could not get over what had just taken place. I started to cry. I felt so helpless.

It wasn't like I was going to leave the flyers up for years, months, or even several weeks.

I was just trying to ask my community for their help in trying to find out where our son was.

What that man and his wife did to me, I would have to say is the cruelest thing that anyone has ever done to me besides the people who took away my son.

I know that this man and woman did not know Darvie. They were just an elderly couple that took walks downtown because after this happened, I started seeing them every once in awhile walking downtown.

A couple of days after the man and woman had done that to me, I saw the man walking on the sidewalk while I was driving down our main street. I drove quickly to the Sonora Police Station that was just around the corner. I ran in frantically thinking that a police officer would be able to quickly run out with me, (like I had seen in the old movies) go stop the man, and tell him that he was not allowed to do that to me.

But what really happened was that there was no police officer available to help me at the time. The receptionist after she had calmed me down for a moment, found out what I was there for and asked me where I had been putting the flyer up at. She advised me that it *was* against the city ordinance to put anything on the poles.

I was so frustrated.

She took my phone number, and a woman deputy did call me later, and she kindly explained to me that as wrong as they thought the people were that had done that to me, it really was against the city ordinance to put it on the poles.

Of course, I was not aware of that at the time that I was taping the flyers up.

What I did not understand though, was that within the week all the Christmas pine wreaths went up, many on the poles, and they stayed there for at least a month.

Farther down the street, someone, who had lost a kitten, had put their flyer up and that flyer stayed on that particular pole for quite awhile.

A couple of months later I had seen the elderly man again walking with his wife, and I had realized that I had blocked that memory of what he had done to me out of my mind, but then just seeing him again brought it all back to me and gave my heart another ache.

I have not seen that elderly couple walking in a long time, and so I do not know what has happened to them.

I have since found out that they are personal friends with a former mayor of our town, which explains some things to me.

Over time, I had people come forward at different times with all kinds of different stories to tell me. Different names of people have been brought up.

I have went to talk to people that I have trusted and had heard that they may know something, but when I have got a hold of them, they tell me that they know nothing.

I have been told things and, at the same time, been told that they will deny everything they ever told me if it ever came back their way.

Another scenario happening at Debby's house was even told to me.

Some stories were so horrible, and I would think, "Well, thank God *all* of these stories cannot be true because they are *all* different scenarios."

And then later on, when I would call the people to ask them for more information about what they had told me, some I never heard back from.

I've also tried to get a hold of other people that knew that they were supposed to get back to me and sometimes a long time goes by before I even hear back from them.

I have also contacted people that knew Darvie and asked them what they knew. Some have responded right away and showed interest in meeting with me and even gave me their phone number, but then when I call them or e-mail them back, they never respond. That has been so frustrating for me.

I always think I sure hope *they* never have a kid missing.

It's like no one wants to get involved, or they are afraid too, or they just don't really care.

One time someone found a femur bone out in the vicinity where we were searching for our son. A person who I knew contacted me about it, and as much as they wanted to help me, the person who found it, turned it in to law enforcement, and that was only as far as they were willing to go with it. Fortunately, it was found to be a femur bone from an animal.

I have sent private messages on Facebook to some men that are in prison or have recently been released from prison that knew Darvie. One person could actually be a person of interest, but I still hope to get a response from all of them one day.

Since I am a mom trying to get answers, my driving force that keeps me going is different from other people. I do not care or fear who is involved.

I still want the guilty ones held responsible. I will do everything that I possibly can to make them accountable for their actions no matter who they are.

I have even had people related to me, write me horrible letters back refusing to help.

Although the three letters that I received back really hurt my heart, I have never responded back to them and I never will.

If I would have responded, I may not have liked the person that I might have become.

There was someone that wrote me a really nasty letter when Darvie was *just* missing, and all I could think after I was done reading it, was either these people are behind his disappearance, or they really are *just this evil.*

Again, I never responded.

One person who I called checking to see if they knew anything got mad at me and hung up on me when I kindly gave them my opinion of who I thought might be behind all of this.

To think that someone would do such a thing, when it was *my* son that was missing at the time.

I have also been told so many things that would have been a lot better for me if I would never have heard them.

There are many things that I have been told that would be too painful to tell my family.

Also another thing people have done is not thought before they have spoken. I think we all are guilty of that at times.

I have had many well-intended acquaintances of mine that when asking me questions or making comments have used words that a mother should never have to hear.

Even our local newspaper was not kind at times, with their pictures or headings regarding articles about our son right after he went missing.

This has broken my heart even more.

I have had neighbors that I felt could have helped get me some needed information from people they know, but they never did help me out.

I was told by someone that Mark had asked them if they had a gun, because he wanted to kill someone.

That same person has told me a scenario of what they say happened to Darvie and then told me who told them the story firsthand. When I checked it out with the other people, who the story supposedly started from, I am told that the *other* person was the one who told the story to *them*.

The only thing I found out from all that information given to me is that I know at least one of them was lying.

But which one could it be? It could possibly be both of them.

All I got was more horrible stuff told to me that I would have to filter through my heart that very likely was all a lie.

The conversations that I have had that have been the most frustrating for me is the ones where the people that I am talking with have said things like, "I heard someone say that they know everything from beginning to end, but I just can't remember who it was." Or, "They told me exactly what happened, but I just can't remember what they said."

Sometimes it was almost too overwhelming for me. It was like I needed to find time to just go somewhere, be able to fall apart, and cry out to the Lord. But so many times, I just tried to handle it all alone.

One person came forward through people I had talked with, took Gloria to a site, and said that they were told that some evidence was thrown over the embankment. Gloria said that the person even shed some tears when she was talking about it.

After I contacted the person, she couldn't give me a straight answer and we eventually checked out the site with the search dogs and found nothing.

One guy named Benny was all *gung ho* on helping me out by going into a few mines at another location that had been part of another scenario. The stories he told me were so unbelievable that it wasn't long before I began to say to myself, *Buddy, I wasn't born yesterday. Even I don't believe you.*

At the very beginning, someone had told me that they had seen a man looking like Darvie in another county recently.

Some other people would see our flyer somewhere, and they would tell me that they were almost positive that they had seen our son.

Another person was at a grocery store and saw Darvie's picture on a flyer when he was just missing. They mentioned to the clerk that they could take down the flyer because our son had died.

The clerk mentioned it to the store manager, and they called the Tuolumne County Sheriff's Office. Then all that day's transactions were checked thoroughly to pinpoint who exactly it was. Since the checker knew what the people had purchased, they were able to locate the people.

But the person really didn't have anything to say to the sheriff's office once he was contacted.

A business owner in town saw our flyer at another business and practically ripped it off the front glass door as he entered the building, and told them arrogantly that they could take it down now.

The employee that worked there knew Darvie well, and she basically told the man that, "They will leave it up as long as they want to", and she taped it back up on the door.

Another time most recently believe it or not, at this same business someone supposedly looked over the flyer for quite awhile and another customer who was there buying something who happened to be a friend of ours noticed. When he confronted the man about it, the man said that he was *almost positive* that this man on the flyer was the same man that he has seen for quite awhile hanging around a utility yard in another town an hour away recently.

Even though we know now that the story could not be possible, for a moment, a very quick moment, we let our minds wander, and we start getting false hope.

Thoughts such as, "*Maybe something happened to him and he got amnesia and he just can't find his way home.*"

But then we remember…

Another thing that happened to me which has stayed with me for a long time and saddened me even now as I think of it, is that a woman named Anita came forward one time who knew Darvie from school years ago.

She had tried to help me it seemed in the beginning with some information. Then a month later she called me up and was asking me if there was still a reward out for someone coming forward with the truth.

She said that she wanted to meet me somewhere to talk with me to tell me what had happened to Darvie.

She said she was afraid to talk on the phone like someone could be tapping the lines so we made plans for her to call me back in a couple of days and we would go meet somewhere.

Anita worked at a local business in town and to act like someone could be tapping the lines and that it might be *unsafe* for her to talk with me from her work phone seemed so silly to me. No one else has ever acted so strange before when it came to giving me information.

Anita never got back to me as planned so I had to hunt her down and call her. She said that she couldn't meet me, but she gave me *kind of a scenario* of what happened over her work phone.

She said her mother had discouraged her from getting involved at all.

Her mother had told her that she had a kid to think about.

She said that she could only give me *some* information, but she would never reveal the person's identity who she had talked to on the street because she had not seen that person for years and she was afraid to tell me anymore.

She only directed me to go look up another guy named Greg that I have so far never found to this day. The detective never looked into this story after I told him about it because he said that the person that she was talking about had already been talked to before by him. I always felt because there was more than one person with the same name that the detective was mistaking that person for someone else that he had already talked with.

After that conversation with her, Anita started acting so strange toward me whenever I would see her at her place of work. I actually went up to her one time and told her that I thought that she was acting like she was trying to avoid me, which she denied.

Now whenever I see her she does not even acknowledge me unless I speak first and then she still acts like she is trying to avoid me. It is just so unbelievable to me the way some people do things.

Even when I saw Linda in town one day, she acted so strange and got away from me as quickly as she could.

Then Darvis at one point started to get prank phone calls on his cell phone.

Sometimes every day or maybe every other day late at night his cell phone would ring.

The calls started out coming from a blocked number. Darvis would answer but no one would be there. It really wasn't like you could hear anyone on it. Darvis would then just hang up.

Eventually the calls would come in where it would say *private* and the same thing would happen. But then another call would come in right after that and have a cell phone number that we would see and then the person would do the same thing. They would call, say nothing and then Darvis would hang up.

Darvis and I both figured it had to do with someone who was part of Darvie's disappearance.

Sometimes the calls would come around midnight or maybe as late as two thirty in the morning. Once in awhile, the calls would come in the day.

This went on for a couple of months, and we even gave the number to Detective Bob who said that he had called it but got no answer. Darvis had even called it, but he too got no answer.

It was silly that they would call, make it say *private*, and then call right back with the number showing, as if we would not realize that it was the same person calling.

One time Darvis called the number right back after the call had come through in the daytime, and a man did answer. When Darvis told him to stop calling, the man said something derogatory to Darvis and hung up.

I kept thinking when is this all going to stop?

I decided that I would do something the next time they called.

One evening after midnight Darvis's phone rang, and I got out of bed and answered it. After no one was on the line, I hung up. I realized that it had said *private* and that I had forgotten to say what I had planned to say to them the next time they called.

I went downstairs for a moment and as I was coming back upstairs to go back to bed, I heard his cell phone ringing again.

I ran up as quickly as I could and as soon as I answered the phone within about five seconds I was able to blurt out, "My son's been murdered, and you are now looking like a suspect, and the sheriff's office would sure love to hear about this."

With that said I hung up.

They have never called back again since.

Thank God.

These are just some of the horrible things that I can remember have happened to me since Darvie went missing.

One saying that I have always said to myself regarding needing help from these people that may know something, and then seeing how they rarely have come through for me is, "They don't really care about what happened to us."

One thing that I believe is that there has been so much evilness throughout all of this for a reason. Right after Darvie went missing, Debby was complaining about her missing occult book to Gloria and a friend named Sam. Debby was arguing with them at the bottom of her driveway while my daughter, Kristie, stood by them. Debby told them that her book had been missing since the sheriff's office entered her home and looked around her place.

Someone had let law enforcement in her house when Debby was not at home.

Debby also collected all kinds of animal bones and skulls for some reason.

I believe that in the spiritual realm that the Bible speaks about, that we do not see with our eyes, there is some kind of spiritual battle going on.

I believe that there are strongholds that need to be torn down,. By my faith in the Lord, and Debby's possible dabbling with the enemy of God, and how the drug scene is such a foothold of the devils, I believe that there is some kind of unseen powers warring against each other.

I do know though that good will always prevail over evil.

That is why in the end, I know the truth will be revealed.

14

Since the very beginning our searches have mainly continued to be at the location where Darvie's clothes were found.

We would search and get discouraged in a never-ending cycle. Not long after we had stopped by and talked with Chuck at his house, we went back up to the property and noticed that the surveillance camera had been put up.

I was always surprised that Chuck did not tell the sheriff's office to let us know that he did not mind if our family went on his property and searched and, for us, not to worry about the surveillance camera.

Instead I began feeling uncomfortable each time we went there searching for Darvie.

I felt like we had enough on our mind and then to have to worry that a landowner may not want us on his property seemed unreal.

We did not trust Chuck at all.

One time Darvis happened to be uptown at a store, and he got a tap on his shoulder, and it was Chuck. He asked Darvis how he was doing.

We were already not feeling good about the things that Chuck had done to Darvie's belongings. It was starting to seem to us now like Chuck could be a person of interest. Darvis turned to him and told him to stay as far away from him as he could. He didn't want anything to do with him.

I guess, one time, when we were up there searching, it was Chuck's day off and he had driven up to the property also. Our truck was parked in the dirt driveway and after Chuck had left the property he called Detective Bob to see if he could ever have a vehicle towed for being up there in his driveway.

A vehicle can't drive anywhere down past the gate anyway, and there is still plenty of room for quite a few vehicles to park up there so I never understood why he would ever have a problem with where we parked.

We have been out on the property so many times. However, there is still a great part of the land out there not owned by Chuck that has never been searched. It could take years to search it all if no one comes forward with the truth.

One time I decided to try to get some character references about Chuck from people that I knew and who worked at the same place as he did.

I called and talked to one man, but he worked a different shift and didn't really know Chuck so he wasn't able to tell me anything.

Then one day I was at a school and I saw a woman, Barbara, who I knew. I had wanted to talk to her because Darvis had told me that her ex-husband worked at the same place as Chuck. I asked her to please try to get a hold of her ex-husband to see if he knew Chuck and if he did, what he thought about him.

After some time had went by, I e-mailed Barbara to see if she was able to get a hold of her ex-husband regarding a character reference about Chuck. I told her if she was not friends with her ex-husband and was not able to ask him that I would understand.

I did not hear back from her until over a week later. When she did e-mail me, she then told me, "I gave him the message. He and

I are best friends for the sake of our son. I can't control what he does with his messages after that".

I felt so frustrated since I really had not gotten any answer from her at all.

So the same day, I e-mailed her again and said that I wanted her to ask him what he *thinks* about Chuck. I asked her to *please* try to find out because this was something important that I needed to know.

I did not hear back from her, but, about a week later as I have seen God do for me many of times, I was driving uptown and there she was right out in front of me waiting to cross the street.

I rolled down my window and asked her if she had received my e-mail because I needed her to ask her ex-husband about what he thought *about* Chuck not just if he *knew* him.

She said she would ask him again and get back to me.

I am always amazed how so many times God has put the right people in my track that I feel like I need to talk to, regarding finding my son.

It always gives me a good feeling.

I think it gives me a little hope that I am moving closer to the truth somehow.

Another week went by and then when Barbara did contact me back through an e-mail, I couldn't believe what she told me.

She said, "After talking to you the other day, I talked to my ex-husband again. Not only did he tell me, but he said "I told you last time you asked what I think of 'Chuckie', that I trust him with my life every day. I would even trust him with our son, our only son. I work with him every day. He has volunteered and taken lie detector tests (which was not true). He told me he feels bad about what's going on and said if her and Darvis or anybody else wants to talk to him, all you have to do is go down there."

She said, "I feel like I kind of got chewed out by my ex-husband for asking again. Then my ex said that from now on that I need to leave him (my ex) out of what's going on. He said he doesn't want the guy stressed out and having it affect his work. He said that the safety of many lives depend on him. He reminded me that he lives right down the road from you. I don't know what else to say. I just hope you can find peace and some answers be brought to light."

Now all I was thinking was, *"Why would a coworker be so defensive? Why couldn't he just say Chuck was a nice guy and leave it at that?"*

I just couldn't believe it.

Something sounded very suspicious to me.

One time as we continued searching, Darvis, Kristie, my stepson David, and I went over an embankment, and we came upon what looked like a whole bunch of animal bones scattered on the hillside. We collected some and put them in small piles.

We also noticed a big rock that was sticking out off of the bank that seemed to make kind of a *cave-like* shelter underneath it for possibly an animal such as a mountain lion we assumed. I had found something that looked like a vertebrae and brought it in to the sheriff's office, but they said that it was most likely from a deer.

We wanted the sheriff's office to come check the location out for us, but it had never been done yet.

Soon after Darvie went missing and after we found his car, we also started searching a couple of other places around the neighborhood where his car had been found because of rumors that we had heard.

One person told us that Darvie had walked up the road with Mark and then he heard a gunshot and when Mark came back, he came back alone. Of course, when I confronted the guy about it, he could not verify exactly what he had seen or heard if anything.

We searched at a vacant house that was above Debby's place. The people who were living there last had moved out right before this all happened, and we had heard that Mark had hung around there after they had moved away.

The house though vacant of people had junk everywhere, inside and outside of the house. Ashtrays filled to the brim with cigarette butts and then piles of cigarette butts just on the floor. Furniture that looked so unsanitary that you would never sit on such a thing. Raw garbage was everywhere. It was so unbelievably filthy.

We have come to know that most of all the houses up there in that area, when people move out, they just leave a lot of the furniture, clothes, garbage, etc. that they no longer want. Even while people are living in the homes, it is very common for raw garbage to be all around the yards in garbage bags just lying around. I don't understand how some people feel like they cannot afford to go to the dump once in awhile and pay less than $20.00 for one truckload. I guess that is why we have seen so many garbage bags just thrown over embankments up in that area. They just don't want to pay the dump fee.

I have been so surprised that people live like this. I have been even more surprised when I see that there are children that have no choice but to live in all of the mess also.

Kristie, when we were up looking around the place had noticed something that looked like a drop of blood on the deck. We put a lampshade that was left on the porch over it. When we left there that day, we went and told Detective Bob, yet no one ever checked the drop of blood out. A year later when we went back out there, we had a hard time trying to figure out where the blood drop had been since of course the lampshade had been removed.

I know that the HRD team came up to this neighborhood and supposedly looked around at this house right after Darvie went missing, yet I have no knowledge if they ever actually came to this particular house.

We have been told by a few people that the drop of blood was there because when Gloria's husband and his friends were moving an air conditioner out of the house, and one of them had cut his finger, he had bled there.

Even Gloria has confirmed that story.

It seemed that our local law enforcement wasn't thinking it was that important to check out the drop of blood probably because of the same reason we were told by so many people *why* it was there.

We were under the impression that our local law enforcement did not have luminal. So Darvis went ahead and purchased some online and had it sent to our home address, but we have never used the luminal yet.

New people had since moved into that house, and we have had so many people insisting that they know why the drop of blood was there. So it has discouraged us to do anything.

After we met with our local sheriff, he told us that he was going to have his detectives check it out even though it was then over two years that Darvie had been missing.

We know someone who works for the person who owns most of those homes up there in that neighborhood. They have given us permission to go anywhere up there at anytime and that the sheriff's office can take up that piece of deck if they feel it is necessary.

A new detective on the case since has said when we inquired about it, that they had checked out that residence and found nothing. He said that after all this time you wouldn't be able to find the drop of blood anyway.

Also when we were searching at that house, we saw a burn pile in the driveway. Debby's boat was also parked up there.

We searched in the back of the place and saw recently-made tire marks in the mud and wondered if Mark had tried to drive back there, up to the road for some reason.

I always wondered if that story was true, the one Kevin had originally told me, and if this was actually the place where Darvie and Mark had argued and where Darvie had escaped out of a window possibly.

This house was also the place where Mark and another man named Greg had been after Darvie had went missing. A woman named Judy had told me that she and her husband had been up there also around that same time.

She said that Greg had two phones in his possession, and one phone had been the same brand as Darvie's had been. She said Greg was acting very strange around them. He had told them supposedly that one phone was used just for texting and one for calling. She asked to use one of them and had actually made a call with it.

I told Detective Bob that story, but he said he did not believe that Greg had the phone anymore as Greg had told him when he had questioned Greg about some things that he had lost his phone. So as far as I know, nothing was ever done to look into that.

Judy was even willing to give me the phone number that she had called on one of Greg's phones if I needed it.

But even with that being told to us, one never knows if that was just another lie told to us.

From the very beginning, the Tuolumne County Sheriff's Office had Darvie's phone pinged constantly. However nothing ever came up on the radar.

Our family continued calling his number and leaving messages for him.

We started at first asking him to please call us.

Then our calls finally were of just us expressing our love to him and our thoughts, as time continued to go by.

Eventually his cell phone service paid only for the current month stopped. Unfortunately awhile after that, his voicemail no longer picked up when we called.

We had tried to figure out his password for the longest time before his service was completely shut off so we could hear any voice mail messages, but we just couldn't figure it out.

When Kristie finally did finally figure the password out which was a miracle in itself, Darvie's phone voice mail was no longer attached to his cell phone number. That just about broke our hearts. We felt like we were so close to maybe hearing something, to only have it slip from our fingers.

But I knew God had his reasons for allowing certain things to go down as they did. I knew that he could still be trusted.

In the seventeen days that Darvie was with us, he kept throwing out passwords to me for some reason. I hardly paid attention, but it was the few times I really listened, that at least gave us some kind of a clue to go with. He also had written down some passwords on a notebook.

There was one time where something had happened regarding us needing one of his passwords that made me cry.

My husband Darvis had to make a very important phone call and get information that we really needed, and the woman representative, on the other end of the phone, would not answer any questions for him unless he could come up with the answer to a specific security question.

Because the representative knew how important it was for Darvis to figure it out, she tried the best she could to help him.

She asked him what the first pet's name of Darvie's was, and Darvis would say, "Of a dog?"

The person kept saying, "His *first* pet's name."

Darvis kept trying to rack his brain to figure out the name of whatever Darvie had figured was his first pet.

What took place next was nothing short of a miracle. Truly it was.

Unbelievably, all of a sudden, it dawned on me.

I remembered…

I spoke not one name, but two names of the first little pets that Darvie had together.

It was his two goldfish that I had gotten him when he was yet a little boy.

The answer was correct.

Something, only a mother would remember.

15

It was so hard to keep up with all the people that we couldn't trust. A few weeks earlier after we had picked up Darvie's car, we were driving by Debby's house with Gloria, and we saw a man named Doug standing in her driveway tinkering with his vehicle.

For some reason Detective Bob had previously questioned Doug about the story that Mark had told, about being up at the property with Darvie and the landowner showing up. Doug told Detective Bob that he had been told that same story by Mark, but it had been a couple of weeks *before* Darvie went missing when he heard it.

I was getting concerned because I knew that Mark had told Gloria that story *after* Darvie went missing, and now Doug was saying that it happened earlier. I just thought that Doug was trying to protect Mark and Debby.

Within a few days after we saw Doug—him and his wife Betty suddenly moved out of their house in this neighborhood and went to the state of New Mexico.

When I heard where they had gone to stay in New Mexico, I realized that I was acquainted with the woman Katrina who they had gone to stay with. In the past, she had lived in this town most of her life too.

Even though I didn't know her that well, I tried to get her to help me out.

When I first e-mailed her I said, "Katrina, boy it truly is a small world! I heard that Doug and Betty are up visiting you. *Please, Please, Please* try to find out all that you can about Darvie's disappearance. They lived right above the house where his car was found (so I thought). They had been around up there when he disappeared, and they *have* to know something. Their stories did not add up when they talked to the detective."

"They said the story that Mark told the detective was told a couple of weeks *before* Darvie disappeared and not *after* he went missing, and that is not true. *Please* Katrina try to find out for me where my son is exactly and who *all* is responsible. Thank you very much".

She responded right away with, "Why do you think I have kept them here for a week? I have asked questions and listened. They are leaving soon. Then I will e-mail you what I feel. So far I really don't think they know anything. I will push harder"

I thanked her and said, "Any information may be the key. God bless you".

I then sent her some questions to ask Doug and Betty if she could.

I never heard back from her.

The short visit that Katrina said that Doug and Betty planned, ended up lasting for almost a year.

A few weeks later I e-mailed her again and said, "Katrina please write me and let me know anything that you found out. It has been a very hard eight weeks. Anything that you have heard could help us. Thank you very much".

She never e-mailed me back.

So feeling so frustrated from not hearing back from her, I just wrote on her Facebook page for all to see.

"Katrina, did you get my e-mail?" She wrote, "They think Mark knows something".

That was it?

That was nothing new to me. Katrina gave me nothing.

About a month later I sent her another e-mail and said, "I do not know why you have not e-mailed me any information regarding anything that Doug and Betty said about my son's disappearance. They had to have said some things to you and all we are doing is waiting to hear anything from anyone. *Our son is missing*!!! Worst nightmare of my life! We keep getting leads, and I feel like we will find him. You told me you think Mark knows something. We have always known that! Mark admits to being with Darvie last. I just do not know why you haven't told me what they have all said to you. Something they said could help us find our son. Anything may help. Thanks."

It didn't take long for me to see, that I was not going to get any help from her at all.

It was so frustrating.

I have never heard back from her again.

One person that I talked with more recently that knows her well, contacted her for me and Katrina told her that she had told me *everything she knew*.

I should have known better than to trust Katrina anyway.

She had never come through for me before.

Right after Darvie had went missing, we put up a bank fund in his name to help us with the reward that we had out and to help us in our search. Katrina had e-mailed me on her own and asked me for my address as she was going to send some money to me the next day.

She never did.

I have always felt like Doug was involved somehow or knew what had happened to Darvie. I believe that he and Betty were hiding out in that other state for a reason.

Especially when I realized that their stay in New Mexico ended up being almost a year than the week visit that was at first planned. When Detective Bob had tried to call Doug a few times and had left messages for him to call him back, he got no response from Doug for quite awhile.

Eventually Doug and Betty came back to this town and Doug finally did contact Detective Bob, but he told the detective he did not know anything about what happened to Darvie.

He said he had only been up at the property (where Darvie's clothes had been found), with Mark a couple of months before Darvie went missing. He said he had not ever been there with Darvie. He said Mark had told him also that it was his grandfather's property and that Mark had been staying on that property off and on for a few months.

I had always thought that Doug and Betty had lived in a house above Debby's house, in another direction than the abandoned vacant house that we had checked out.

However it wasn't until recently that I found out that they had actually lived in a house on another road in the same neighborhood—the same exact road where Maria had lived at the time and where Mark's truck had been found, which now, has made me even more suspicious of them.

If something had happened in Maria's house close to where Doug and Betty had been living and they had been brought into a situation somehow, that would give all the reason in the world for them to quickly leave town.

I have heard from their acquaintances that they left their house with all of their things still in it and never came back to get any of it. They told me that when they said they left everything, they mean *everything*!

We had previously checked out Maria's house on the outside, and now we were at the house again.

Louie had mentioned going to Maria's house after he had ran away from Mark, when he felt like Mark had tried to poison him. It was also the same house that the woman Linda had told us about. Maria was nowhere to be found as she had moved out of the house right around the time Darvie had gone missing, and new people were now living there. Darvis and I told the people that we had permission from the property owner, (which we had), to look over the property.

The first time we had went out to the house, Darvis and I went down the bank and looked around. There was a horse carcass over the embankment that had been there awhile.

We have been told that Debby had mentioned in the past that she had wanted the horse carcass to add to all her collection of bones but had never came to get it.

Now this second time that we were at the house, we brought a few friends with us. We all looked around, and the guys went into the hills behind the house, but none of us found anything.

Every time that we would see tarps or blankets or containers or bags, we would turn them over, open them up, and check them out.

I wish now that I would have gone inside the house after Maria had moved out since many people have lived there since.

At one time, even Louie had moved in the house for awhile but has since moved out. That even seemed strange to me when I heard that.

I think the reason why we never pushed to go inside the house was that we must have not really believed that story. Maybe we just didn't *want* to believe it.

We had waited to hear from the person that we knew that handles the rentals for the landlord in this neighborhood. They had told me that we could go inside and look around the house whenever it became vacant again.

The problem is that once someone moves out whether they are paying rent or not, someone else moves right in behind them.

We had been told we could even tear up the carpet if we needed to.

I really wanted to get some search dogs over in that area as the dogs had not been able to check it out yet because there was always someone living in it. The search dogs were only supposedly taken to this neighborhood over at the abandoned vacant house that was above the road where Debby lives, not at this house where Maria had lived.

But because we just did not know if our suspicions meant anything or not in this neighborhood, eventually we turned our thoughts back to the property where Darvie's clothes had been found that was about five miles away.

We knew that we at least should start there.

So we decided to plan a community search.

16

To plan for our search, we called our local newspaper. We wanted to let them know ahead of time that we were going to have a search and to ask if they would put that information in their paper so that we could ask our community to help us.

We were very encouraged by doing this because it felt good to make plans to have other people get on board with us. We knew that we needed them. It gave us some hope.

The Tuolumne County Sheriff's Office had wanted to have another search of their own, but they were not able to have one this particular weekend so that is why we went ahead and planned our search. We were very anxious to get one done.

The article regarding our search came out in our local newspaper two days before we were actually going out.

The evening the article came out in the paper Chuck actually called our house and I answered the phone. He mentioned the search to me and asked me, "Where are you guys going to be searching?"

I told him to hold on and then I gave the phone to Darvis. I felt uncomfortable that Chuck was calling and hoped everything would work out.

Chuck asked Darvis the same question and then told him, "If you guys are going to be on my property, I might have a problem with that."

Darvis said, "You shouldn't have a problem with it if you don't give anyone permission, because if someone gets hurt, they would be trespassing."

Chuck told Darvis, "Well Jim (another neighbor that lived down below) and I are going to go up there tomorrow and look around."

With that, the call was ended.

After Darvis hung up the phone and told me what Chuck had said, all I could think was "Why, so he can move evidence?"

After our search, Jim, the neighbor, called us and left a message saying that he was sorry that he hadn't gone and helped out on the search, but that he had hurt his leg. I have never found out if he had actually gone up to the property the day before with Chuck, and maybe hurt his leg then or if he never even knew anything about Chuck wanting him to go up with him and never did.

The night before our search, Kristie and I had expressed to Detective Bob that we just felt like we were *wasting our time* going out there to the property. We were thinking, "What if his clothes were just left there to keep us looking in the wrong area?" The detective said, "If only to *rule it out*, that would be a good enough reason to have the search there."

We knew he was right.

We heard from lots of friends that they would be joining us for the search. We had other friends call us to tell us that they were not going to be able to make it, but wished that they could.

Even strangers who had gotten our phone number from the article in the paper had called us to ask directions to where we were all going to meet up.

We told everyone to meet up at the top of the main road first thing the next morning and then we would all go down together.

Now I couldn't wait. I was so glad that we had finally planned a search where our community was going to help us out.

Saturday, January 15, 2011

Early on this morning we drove up to the location where we were going to meet everyone. It wouldn't be long and they would all be there soon.

Darvis and I, Kristie and Bobby, and my niece Dawn were waiting around talking when all of a sudden who comes driving in but *Chuck*!

We had no idea that Chuck had planned to be up on the property while we did our search. Now seeing him and realizing that he was actually here, brought anxiety to us all.

Obviously, he wanted to be on his property when people started showing up.

Was it possible to oversee everything and everywhere that we were going?

Our daughter Kristie decided that she and Bobby should drive down to the property. She would try to talk to Chuck and explain to him that it really wasn't a good idea for him to be there with all of us. She would assure him that no one was going to be taking anything off of his property. She would explain that we just needed to search for her brother.

While Kristie was talking to Chuck, she said she started asking him questions. She asked him what he knew about what happened around the time Darvie went missing. She wanted to see what his story would be.

Kristie said it was strange though because Chuck kept getting his days mixed up and changing his story even as he told it to her. She had a deep sense of unease as he spoke to her sensing he was telling her lies.

When I later mentioned Chuck's confusion about the days in his story to the Tuolumne County Sheriff's Office, it didn't seem to make a difference to them at all.

As the time arrived for everyone to meet, we were standing alone, just my family. Anxiety started to fill our minds as we worried that no one would show up. We didn't voice our concerns, but sadness and fear was evident in our faces. Then, suddenly, we heard vehicles coming up the road. Smiles broke out on our faces as car loads of people started showing up. We had friends, strangers, and acquaintances to help in the search. Some people came alone and others came with friends. Tears ran down our faces as people waved at us and cheered us on as they found parking. After searching, often alone, for months for our loved one, this show of support overwhelmed us…finally others would help us in searching for Darvie.

It was so evident to us how God was blessing us. It felt so good to see the support that we were getting from everyone.

When we were all gathered, Darvis and I spoke out loud to everyone to explain what our plan was. Our pastor who had came to help in the search prayed for us as we were all joined together in a big circle.

By the time our pastor was done praying and I opened my eyes, I realized then that I was the only person still standing in the road. Unbeknownst to me, someone had drove back up the road and was waiting for me to move so he could go by.

It was Chuck…

Kristie had done what she had set out to do. She had convinced Chuck that it was best if he didn't stay. He was now leaving and going back home.

That was such a burden lifted off of us. I was so thankful to the Lord!

We then all started caravanning down the long road.

Darvis and I led the way as people had climbed up in the back of trucks including our truck to hitch a ride down to the location that we were headed to.

We met Kristie and Bobby down at the entrance of the property. As they stood there watching and as we parked and were able to also watch all the vehicles coming down the road, it filled our hearts with so much gratitude.

People really did care and wanted to help us look for our son.

A couple of things we did notice after we got up to the property this time was that Chuck had put a whole bunch of 'No Trespassing' signs all around on trees beside the road past his dirt driveway, and he had also painted over the part on the gate that said "You Will Bleed". Obviously he did not want any of the people coming on the search to see what he had originally written. If you looked real close you could still read it underneath the paint.

Our plan was for us all to walk down together to the lower mine. It was quite a journey to walk down to it, about a quarter of a mile. We would then spread out like ten to twenty feet apart once we got down there and then start working our way down toward the creek another one hundred fifty yards.

After Darvis and I got down to the lower mine, we looked up. Seeing all the people walking in a row, one in front of the other, coming down the trail to the lower mine was amazing.

Our hearts were overflowing with so much gratitude and appreciation.

This was the first time being on this property, that our search would take us down to the creek.

Being told the area had already been searched had made us never think of going down close to the water's edge.

But this time we did…

My niece Dawn and I were part of a group that started going off toward the left and then down the embankment. There were only a few people ahead of us that had started going more to the left and down before we did.

It wasn't long after we started to climb down the mountain that for some reason I said out loud forgetting my earlier doubts, "God, I just know you have us right where you want us to be."

It wasn't ten minutes later when, John, one of our friends, came running over from my left, and he told me, "We found something!"

17

John wanted to know where Darvis was, and I told him, "Back over on my right, just a little ways".

With anticipation, my niece Dawn and I waited for him to locate Darvis. As soon as they got back to us, we all quickly went over together to see what they had found.

The area we were brought over to was only about one hundred yards away from where my niece and I had been and about twenty feet above the water's edge.

As soon as we arrived, right out in the open lying on the ground was something I will never forget.

It was a lower mandible.

A lower mandible, without any teeth.

Knowing Darvie had worn dentures, many questions began running through my mind.

I really don't think I was able to actually grasp what I was seeing and experiencing.

I don't think that I could let my mind, let alone my heart do that. I was so confused.

With about five or six people all around, we tried to figure out exactly what we were looking at.

Was it animal or human remains?

How did it get there?

With gloves and a plastic bag, my poor sweet husband carried it all the way up to the top of the mountain. We had to find cell service to call Detective Bob.

Carrying these remains out will haunt my husband forever.

Word had spread quickly on the mountain so many people were now climbing back up to the top to join us.

After we had called the detective, it didn't take long for him to show up.

He took the plastic bag from Darvis and put it in a safe secure place.

Though we had a long way to travel back down the mountain, Darvis, Kristie, and I, took the detective to show him exactly where it had been found. This time, we hiked straight down the mountain through all the congested brush.

We finally made it back down to the location. We all spread out and continued searching in the general area where the bone had been found.

Even though what was found was far above the water, Kristie noticed something that was camouflaged in the leaves beside the water's edge.

She bent down wondering what it was since it didn't seem to fit in the natural setting. It appeared to be gum. As she reached out to touch the object, she realized it was a bone fragment. With horror, she pointed it out to the detective, and he was able to retrieve it.

It was indeed a small piece of bone of some kind.

As we got back up to the road again, we reluctantly gave Detective Bob the name of Darvie's dentist that he had gone to years ago while still living in Sonora. He needed that information so he could contact the dentist to check our son's dental records.

With a heavy heart, we all went home.

18

On our way home reflecting on the day that we had just experienced, we were so grateful to everyone for the support they gave us.

There had been so many people walking the land searching for anything that they could find. It meant so much to us.

Our minds and our bodies were on overload, and we were emotionally drained. All I wanted to do was go to sleep and never wake up again.

The next day with sad anticipation we waited to hear from Detective Bob.

Toward evening, he came to our house, and he wasn't there very long before he confirmed what we had already known in our hearts.

The exact match with the comparison of several of Darvie's dental records could not be denied.

Our hearts were absolutely broken.

Our son was really gone and he wasn't coming back!

19

It was so hard to deal with the reality of what we had just found. It seemed like God himself had put what we had found right out in the open for us to find.

We felt like it was maybe to let us know the things that we needed to know.

Search dogs had supposedly already been down there from the very beginning. Detective Bob said the search teams GPS missed it by ten feet. Another time, I was told one hundred feet.

We now began to look at some things differently.

We believed God's hand was definitely in it because what we had found was truly something very important in identifying someone. At least we realized that God wanted us to know that Darvie was no longer with us. Darvie was resting safely in his loving care where no one would be able to hurt him anymore.

It was as if God had stepped in and with him knowing how hard of a life Darvie had always had, said "*Enough!*"

The next day, the Tuolumne County Sheriff's Office had another dog come out and comb the area some more. A few more small bone fragments were found along the water edge. But that was it.

A couple of days after that, the sheriff's office had a man in a wetsuit search all day upstream and downstream in the creek for quite a distance, but nothing was found.

We continued our search there in the days that followed. As horrible as it seemed, the more we searched, the more we hoped to find something. And it was '*our son*' we were hoping to find. It was really more than we could bear to think about.

Soon afterward, Darvis happened to find a long crowbar lying on the mountainside over the embankment just behind the two trailers that were up above on the property. It was around the place where Darvie's sweatshirt had been found.

It was an item that seemed out of place.

Kristie and Darvis noticed that it looked like some kind of substance was on the crowbar.

It was given to law enforcement for them to check it out. They then came back and said that the crowbar had some wax on it like the wax from the candle that was found in the trailers up above.

The crowbar has never been checked for DNA, fingerprints, etc.

Almost two years after Darvie went missing our local sheriff himself, had never even heard about the crowbar before, until Darvis mentioned it to him. He said that he was going to see if it could be checked out more thoroughly.

We have never heard anything more about it.

If you continued hiking all the way straight down from where the crowbar had been found near the water below, that is where we found our son's remains.

After getting the bone fragments checked out, Detective Bob said that a physician had told them that what we had found would have been from a frontal fracture.

(A frontal fracture means fractures that can be caused by blows to the head as well as falls on hard surfaces or against sharp and hard objects. It can cause pretty serious damage to the brain especially to the eye and nose area.)

There was not a trace of animal marks on the remains that were found.

We continued to say that we wanted the landowner Chuck to take a lie detector test.

But in the past every time we mentioned it, it was as if the detective didn't think it was necessary.

I felt like no one was listening to us when it came to the landowner.

Eventually Detective Bob did finally bring it up to Darvis that he too wanted Chuck to take a lie detector test.

We were so ecstatic! We again had some hope!

We were so thankful to the Lord that someone had finally listened to us.

Little did we know, it would be at least a year before a lie detector test was finally set up.

20

Our family knew that soon we would want to make plans to have a service to celebrate Darvie's life. Kristie and I started to plan for the celebration and how we wanted to honor Darvie.

Darvis and I contacted a church that we had attended for a long time in the past about having the service there. They were so kind and worked everything out for us in the way that we wanted Darvie's service to be.

With a sad heart, Kristie and I prepared two poster size picture collages of Darvie. Some were of him alone, and some were pictures of other family members taken with him from when he was a baby to a grown adult. The people who attended his service would then be able to look at them and see how special Darvie was to so many people.

Saturday, February 5, 2011

The big church was packed with so many family and friends.

Darvie's younger sister Kerri got up and read a beautiful poem that she had written for him.

Then Darvie's best friend Kathy got up and spoke about the special relationship that they had always had ever since they were in elementary school.

Our daughter Kristie then spoke and gave a wonderful tribute to her brother. She told of many things that we had been going through for almost the past four months. She spoke the words that had been expressed so tenderly from Darvis and I as we had been going through this nightmare. She finished by reading a poem that I had just written for his service called "My Biggest Fan."

Bobby sang two songs "Photographs and Memories" by Jim Croce, and "Homesick" by MercyMe. He sang them wonderfully.

The pastor gave a great sermon for us all to hear.

Before the service started and also after it was over, we had so many family and friends standing in line to give us hugs and encouraging words. I have never felt so loved.

We were given some houseplants and flowers that day, and we continue to see the hand of God through these plants and flowers, even now almost four years later. It is amazing, as they continue to bloom each year.

One small Hydrangea plant that we received is in a barrel in our backyard and has grown so big and continues to bloom around fifty flowery bunches at a time. It is just beautiful with four different colors.

A Blue Buddleia Butterfly bush was given to us that we also planted in our backyard in a barrel. The words that were written in the card that came with it, said "When the butterflies come, you can think of your son".

That really touched my heart and made me cry.

As the plant begun to bloom with beautiful flowers, Darvis and I started watching for the butterflies. We never saw any around the plant though until Darvis caught sight of a big monarch butterfly that had landed,. He was able to capture that picture with his camera.

We were so grateful to the Lord how he continued to touch our hearts in ways like this that meant so much to us.

After we had spotted the big monarch butterfly, we transplanted the bush from the barrel to the ground. We must not have transplanted it at the right time because it suddenly died and nothing we did could make it survive. We were so disappointed.

So we just recently got another Blue Buddleia Butterfly bush in Darvie's memory and the butterflies have already started to come.

Again, another blessing has come our way.

Someone else gave us a Rose of Sharon tree, and what was so unbelievable to us happened the very first year that we had the tree. The evening before Darvie's birthday while I was out of town, Darvis called me crying saying that a flower for the first time ever was starting to bloom on the tree. The one flower bloomed the whole day of his birthday and the day after his birthday it was completely gone. There was no trace of any flower left.

The next year about a couple of weeks before his birthday, Darvis and I unbeknownst to each other had been watching the tree. We were waiting to see what would happen. When I eventually mentioned it to Darvis, he acknowledged that he too was watching just as I was to see if it was going to bloom.

Again we were amazed. The day of his birthday, a flower was getting ready to bloom.

I always felt like it was the Lord telling us that everything was going to be okay.

What is again unbelievable is what I have seen as I have been writing this chapter. The Rose of Sharon tree for the first time ever, even though it is still a little over a month before Darvie's birthday, as I just walked outside I have noticed, a flower has bloomed.

21

After being in the local county jail for a while, Mark eventually was transferred to prison because of a prior warrant. Darvis continually asked the detective to please go, see Mark, and question him some more.

The trip would only take a little over an hour to get there. Darvis even offered to pay for the gas. We just wanted the Tuolumne County Sheriff's Office to make more contact with Mark.

We wanted the prison to know the importance of them helping us find out what happened to our son. We were hoping that maybe through a cellmate, we could get some answers.

We felt so much frustration in trying to find the truth.

Detective Bob told Darvis that Mark wasn't *going anywhere*, so I guess he thought he had plenty of time to go down and talk to Mark.

Unfortunately about two months later and less than five months after Darvie died, I got a call from someone who had heard something on the street that morning.

Mark was dead!

22

We were so shocked with the news regarding Mark's death. One of the main *persons of interest* had now met his maker.

Many people we encountered regarding his death kept saying to me that now our chances of learning the truth were gone.

I refused to believe that.

I knew God did not make mistakes, and I would not believe that we were suddenly at a dead end.

We found out Mark had come down with a life threatening infection and had only a couple of weeks to get his life in order. I was told even Debby was allowed to go see him.

I am not sure if the detective had any knowledge of Mark's illness ahead of time or not, but regardless he never saw Mark. Law enforcement told us that Mark never recanted his previous statements or gave any new information out to anyone. Mark would never be able to answer our many questions.

No matter what part Mark played in my son's death, I was not happy over someone else losing their life.

With Mark's death, we now hoped for someone, someone like Louie, to come forward with information. Since Mark was dead maybe someone would now tell us the whole story. We even thought it would give someone who might have been a part of our son's death or at least knew exactly what had happened, a perfect opportunity to come forward. We were thinking they would say that Mark had told them everything and just blame it all on Mark.

Unfortunately, no one came forward to tell the truth.

So now as it were, Mark and Louie, two of three people, that we felt were involved either in Darvie's death or at least knew what happened had died or had almost died.

I couldn't understand why this was happening.

I did not believe in a thing called Karma even though so many people have brought that up to me.

But I knew that we *reap what we sow* according to God's Word.

I also knew that in the Bible it says in Ezekiel 18:23 (King James Version), *"Have I any pleasure at all that the wicked should die? saith the Lord God: and not that he should return from his ways, and live?"*

I knew all God wants, is for us all to turn from our sinful ways and come to repentance before it is too late.

I also knew the enemy of God was behind all of this somehow.

The enemy uses people for his wicked ways and hates us all, and so he has no concern that our end might be eternal damnation and separation from the almighty God. A God who loves us all so much that he sent his only Son to die for us to pay the penalty for our sins if we would just accept his free gift.

All I could think was, "Father, please forgive them for they know not what they do".

23

Since we have not known the actual truth of what happened to Darvie from the very beginning, we have had to go from one group of persons of interest to another group of persons of interest and yet still know that the two groups are not even connected.

It has been so very frustrating not getting many answers. It has been very hard to have to go through different scenarios in our mind, but I knew I couldn't give up.

In time because of the uncertainty of everything that was going on and the mistrust that we felt from almost everyone we encountered, we began having doubts about what was inside a particular mine on Chuck's property. It was the bottom mine where water continually flowed out of it.

The same mine that one of the HRD dogs had acted a little different around.

It was the mine that Louie told us had another room in it. We had some other people go into the mine for us. When we asked them if there was a room inside the mine that you could go in and stand up in, they too said there was.

Eventually a woman, Shawna had gone inside the mine with the other guys and finally told us that there was no room. No room at all.

Darvis wanted to see for himself, what was in the mine. So Darvis and Kristie decided that the next time we went up to the property they would go into the mine together.

Mines have always frightened me so I knew that I would not be going in one.

Soon we went back to the property, and Darvis and Kristie went inside the mine. Bobby and I waited outside the entrance.

The two of them went all the way to the back of the mine where it finally ended about 125 yards. They searched it very well, but they did not find anywhere in the mine that they could go into another room.

About a week later Darvis and I waited at the entrance and this time, Bobby and Kristie went in. They wanted to see if they could go in farther up in the mine but they couldn't.

We were so discouraged to know that there were so many people that we just couldn't trust.

Then another surprise came our way.

We found out that Debby had been rushed to the hospital and had almost died from a severe infection. She had to have emergency surgery. She was in the hospital for at least a month and according to a friend of hers, she has never been the same.

A couple of weeks after Debby got released from the hospital Detective Bob went to see Debby again. He wanted to see after this *near death* experience if maybe she had decided to finally talk.

She told him that *now* she had a hard time remembering anything.

Was that the truth or just a convenient excuse?

24

Three *persons of interest* in one of the groups of people that we had suspected may be responsible for our son's death or at least knew what happened were now dead or had almost died.

After Darvis and Kristie had gone into the mine and before we even felt like Louie was a person of interest, I had called a relative of Louie's named Deanna. Deanna was a casual acquaintance of mine from years ago and who was a possible friend with Darvie. I told her Louie had not told us the truth about the mine, and I was wondering if she could call Louie and ask him if he would take us up to the site. I wanted Louie to show us exactly the mine that he was talking about.

I have always wondered why law enforcement never took Louie up to the property to make him show them what he was talking about when he described being up there with Mark.

All Deanna kept saying was Louie was afraid. She said he had already told Detective Bob everything, but she was sure Louie would talk to us again if we really needed him to.

She also kept saying how wonderful Debby was, and how Debby had almost died, and that Debby was just *so meek* now that she had been so sick.

Not once did Deanna express any concern or caring toward me, regarding me losing my son.

Now overwhelmed by the conversation where I did not get the help I had expected, and with suspicions that I was starting to have regarding Louie's involvement, made it now seem like it would just be a waste of time to even try to contact Louie.

A few days later, I saw Debby and Deanna driving around together like they had no worries in the world. Just seeing them and knowing that at least one of them, or perhaps both of them knew what happened to my son, and yet they still didn't care made me feel like I had to gasp for air. Overwhelmed, the tears began to fall.

Now thinking back to the landowner of the property, we continued to press the detective to see when Chuck, was going to get to take his lie detector test.

We even offered to pay for it.

The detective kept saying that he was just waiting for the right time. He said he had to wait until the guys, who would give the lie detector tests (to hopefully Louie) and (to Chuck), would be available.

Waiting for the right moment for the tests to be taken felt like an eternity to me. We were so anxious waiting to even see if Louie and Chuck would really actually *take* the lie detector test when finally it was scheduled.

Detective Bob agreed with us that Chuck kept acting like he was never down at his property, when other people were ever around. Although when we looked at the timeline of when Chuck said he did everything, it was a time when Mark and possibly Darvie were down there on the property.

If people had been going down on Chuck's property for a while and Chuck had actually written all those things on his gate and bulldozer a couple of months earlier, it seemed that he was aware of what was going on at his property. For Chuck to say that he had *never* encountered *anyone* the whole time he was going out there checking out things seemed to me that he was not telling the whole truth. As obsessed that Chuck seemed to be, he had to have words spoken with *someone* at one time or another.

I knew there had to be more to the story, but who could I get to believe the same way as I did? I felt so defeated because I felt like law enforcement was not listening to me.

If things were going on for a while at Chuck's property, but it was *only* when Darvie went missing that Chuck *ever* found anything and *then* decided to do what he did, is too hard for me to ever believe.

Sometimes I wonder if Chuck is the guilty one, did Darvie end up getting Chuck's wrath against Mark?

25

The days seemed endless as we waited for the lie detector tests to take place.

As we were waiting for that day to come, I received a call from a friend of Darvie's named Melissa. She told me that Bill, a friend of hers, told her what *really* happened to Darvie. Her girlfriend didn't want her to say anything to anyone but Melissa felt that I needed to know.

I had to quickly distance myself from what Melissa was beginning to tell me as I took pen to paper to write it all down. I was not completely grasping how horrible the scenario sounded that she was telling me. I couldn't let myself think that it was *my son* that we were talking about.

No matter how awful it would be, if what she was telling me was the truth, it still seemed to make more sense than some of the other things that I had heard. This scenario involved six people. Debby, Mark, Louie, Doug and Betty. She didn't know who the sixth person was. I was thinking the last extra person is always missing!

As the conversation came to an end and I hung up, I fell to my knees sobbing. It was almost unbearable the mixed emotions that I was feeling. I did not want any of what I had just been told to have happened to my son, and yet all I wanted was the *truth*. The truth from *someone*! *Anyone*! Was the truth too much to ask for?

I grasped at everything I had just heard like a person reaching for something in complete darkness to tell me that *finally* we would know the truth.

I sprang to my feet to go tell Darvis, and then I quickly called Detective Bob to tell him what I had been told. I gave him Melissa's name and number for him to call her.

Detective Bob always made time for us. I will forever be grateful of all that he did for us as often as he was able to.

Ironically, the next afternoon before I had time to dissect all the new information that I was given, Gloria called Darvis and told him that she was bringing over a guy named Bill who was going to tell us what happened to Darvie.

After Darvis told me that Gloria had called, I again went into our bedroom and just collapsed on my knees to the Lord sobbing. I knew Gloria and Melissa had not been talking and so I was thinking everything was all coming together. We were *really* going to find out the truth. Thank you God! There would be no more waiting!

We were full of anticipation as the detective arrived, first.

Gloria and Bill arrived shortly afterwards.

Bill seemed like a nice guy, and it seemed to me that he was eager to tell us what he knew.

Gloria went outside to wait until we were done. The four of us sat in our living room. I was impatient as small talk began between us, but eventually the detective knew what had to get done, and so he began to ask Bill questions. We began to listen.

Bill started by telling a completely different story than what I had been told the night before by Melissa. What he had supposedly told Melissa's friend was not the things that he was saying. When I asked him who else he had told this story to, he said as he was pointing outside, "Only Gloria."

Now knowing that was not the truth, discouragement began to settle in. I felt like I could just scream.

Bill began to move around in his seat and began to appear uncomfortable. Seeing the way that he was starting to act, the detective asked Bill if he would feel more comfortable with Darvis and I being out of the room, and he kindly said yes.

So a little reluctantly I got up. Just wanting the truth to be told to the detective was important enough if we had to step outside.

Darvis and I visited with Gloria as Bill and Detective Bob continued talking for maybe an hour more.

We were so grateful to Gloria for what she was trying to do for us. She seemed truly wanting to help us find the truth.

Small talk, a hug, and a handshake from Bill were all we received after the detective was done talking to him. Then Gloria and Bill drove away.

We couldn't wait to hear what the detective had to say. But much talk, he did not do. He really didn't have much to say to us which surprised me.

I figured he just wanted to go back to his office and look over all his notes and try to make sense of it all before he gave us his opinion. We thanked him and he was on his way.

We eventually found out that Bill told the detective that he needed to talk to a guy named Dave who was in prison and had been in prison when Darvie had gone missing. In turn, Dave told the detective that a guy named Keith is who he needed to speak with.

I don't believe that law enforcement ever did find Keith though.

More recently, I was taken somewhere by a girl named Megan to speak to another woman who told me that Dave definitely knew what happened to Darvie. But Dave is still in prison. He had been released from prison for a short time but ended up getting in trouble again. I always wondered if he had gotten himself in trouble for a reason. Did he know more than the sheriff's office thought he did?

In time, Darvis and I got to know Bill a little bit more. Bill would now stop by once in a while wanting to go up behind our house in the mountains to ride his off-road vehicle.

Whether I was gone at the time when Darvis told me he had stopped by or if I was just leaving in my vehicle as I saw him arrive, it always bothered me because I felt like Bill was forgetting that our whole lives had been turned upside down. All I cared about was finding Darvie. I didn't care that he wanted to go riding on the property behind our house with no more said to me about our son.

I called Bill one time to ask him some questions. Bill told me that one night when Louie was drunk, he said he knew exactly what happened to Darvie.

I was horrified to hear that and for a couple of months what he had told me weighed on me so heavily it was almost all I ever thought about.

I didn't want to upset my husband so I did not tell him what I had heard. I had my remaining family to think about.

I eventually called Bill back again and asked him if he would please give me more information about the things that Louie had said. Bill just made a bunch of excuses of why he couldn't do that just yet.

He said that he would have to go about it a certain way, when the right time came about.

I felt all alone talking with people constantly who seemed to really care less about my loss.

Bill has never really told us a story that brought us closer to the truth. No matter how nice he was to me, or how much he seemed to want to help, talking with Bill I never knew if he was telling the truth or telling me a bunch of lies.

With the flyers on my car's back passenger windows, every once in a while people would stop and talk to me and tell me that they knew Darvie or had heard something about what had happened. I listened to each and every one of the stories that anyone would tell me.

I was a mother on a mission who wanted justice for my son.

One day in November 2011, I just happened to be on a side street turning around in my vehicle, and I saw a woman who I did not know but I had always seen walking around town. She was walking my way. As soon as I backed up, I noticed her coming toward my car pointing at the flyer on my car window. When I rolled down my window she pointed at the flyer and asked me if I knew him. When I told her that he was my son, she asked me if I knew what had happened to him. I told her that I had heard lots of stories. She again asked me, "But do you know the *real* story?"

She proceeded to tell me where to go and told me to speak to a couple named Kara and Paul, who lived there. She told me to tell them that Pam had sent me and to tell them that she said for them to tell me the *real* story. As she began crying, she walked away.

I was so caught up in the moment that I had quickly forgotten the names that she had just told me. I drove by her and asked her again what her name was and if she could tell me again the other names that she had mentioned.

She repeated all the names to me and included a relative of hers where I could stop by in the same area and find out from them where exactly Kara and Paul lived.

I thanked her and as I started driving away she stood on the sidewalk, put her face in her hands and sobbed.

That sight has never left me.

If I take too long and dwell on this story, it will always bring me to tears.

This is just another example of how I feel I have seen God's hand bringing people in my path at the right time, giving me new information and possibly more needed information as I have journeyed along trying to find the true answers.

I was afraid to bring my husband to go talk to Kara and Paul. Fear of what might take place when I encountered this couple was the reason I sought to find someone else.

Through the coaxing of my daughter Kristie reminding me that it would be better if Darvis came along, I asked Darvis to come with me. Within a day, Darvis and I went and found where the couple lived. We had stopped at the relative of Pam's just like Pam had said to do. The neighborhood was more of a run-down mobile home park. I was nervous as we were driving over. I wasn't quite sure which mobile home it was, yet it wasn't hard to figure out which one it was once we got there. It had trash everywhere and junk piled all around.

Someone came out and walked away. I got out of our vehicle and headed toward the place. Another person came out and was leaving and I asked them if Kara or Paul were there. They said Paul was so I motioned for Darvis to get out of his truck and I knocked on the door. When I found out it was Paul who answered the door, I introduced myself and told him Pam had sent me and she said they could tell me the *real* story.

I had so much hope that Paul would finally tell me what we needed to know.

But, instead, Paul told me I shouldn't believe anything that Pam said.

He said Pam was a crazy woman. A couple of other people came out and confirmed the same thing. Pam wasn't anyone that you should believe. Paul brought up Louie's name without me saying a word and even brought up a distant relative of mine that I did not really know and said he had told them that, "Louie couldn't have killed him because Louie had already been questioned and had never been arrested."

It wasn't long before I realized that this guy was a friend of Louie's because he mentioned that Louie was now back in town. I could tell he wasn't about to act like he knew anything. I said to him, "I am just waiting for the missing key to find out the truth."

I thanked him for talking with me and then Darvis and I drove away.

I had not received what I had been looking for. I was so sure my questions would be answered.

The more I thought about it, I realized that I had not once even mentioned Louie to Paul, or let Paul know he had mentioned a distant relative of mine as he spoke. As far as he knew, Pam had told me everything.

I had not let on Pam had told me nothing more than to talk to him. It seemed like I was on to something, but I didn't know what exactly.

I knew that now I had to find Pam to tell her I hadn't received any information at all. I would need for her to tell me what she knew.

I tried to find out how to get a hold of her, but I couldn't get any help from people that knew her.

I would have to wait for the Lord to see him come through for me like he always did and bring other people in my path that would lead me again to her.

It would be a long time before our paths would ever cross again.

26

I didn't know how we were ever going to be able to get the answers that we so much needed to be able to find out the truth.

I knew that I couldn't rely on law enforcement to be working on the case like they had at the very beginning. Unfortunately crimes continued to take place and they had to give the more recent cases priority.

I knew though that I could rely on the Lord to lead us. He would be the one to set us free.

One day Darvis and I were up at the property where Darvie's clothes had been found. Right in front of the run-down trailers I found a bone just lying on the ground. Then when I turned over a wooden step, there was another small piece of something that also looked like a bone.

I thought that it was so strange to see a bone just out there lying on the ground and to find possibly another bone underneath a step, since we had been up in the area so many times before. I put both bones in a bag and took them home. I held onto them for a couple of months.

I was afraid to give them to the sheriff's office to find out if they were human bones. I did not know if the bones would really be examined, as I was afraid that the sheriff's office would decide the bones were not important. I decided to call the local college to see if they could check the bones out for me. They referred me to a bigger college about fifty miles away where a forensic doctor taught. I called and left her a message. She did call me back and said she would be willing to look them over, but she also said she had to have law enforcement involved to be able to do it. I understood her reason.

I just didn't want to release them to anyone. For so long I felt like I might have found something! I wanted to hold on to them just in case…I felt like I had some hope to hold on to before I actually had to find out the truth, one way or another. It is weird how you can make all kinds of things into what you want them to be. For a while, at least it seems…

27

With more determination, we decided to put another article in our local newspaper. We wanted to let the community know that we were now offering a $25,000 reward to anyone leading us to the rest of our son's remains.

The article also stated that we may be looking into contacting a private investigator in the near future and also may eventually contact additional media.

Within a few days a former police officer from a county nearby, contacted me, and offered his service to us free of charge.

He was now doing private investigating and wanted to see if he could help us out.

I was ecstatic that someone was going to try to help us.

He met us within days and seemed to check out things that no one had ever really looked at before. He even put on gloves as he looked through some of Darvie's possessions. I liked that he was being very professional.

He checked out a GPS that Darvie had used in his car to see if there was anything unusual put on it.

Oh, how I hoped, there would be something on it!

We couldn't get out to my car fast enough to check it out.

Unfortunately Darvie had only tracked his trip coming down from Oregon.

The private investigator looked over the restraining orders that Darvie had received. I looked over the restraining orders myself, and remembered how Darvie had been preparing his own restraining order against someone who had been causing all kinds of trouble for him in his marriage.

Since Darvie always tried to believe the best in people, he took the bait as they buttered him up, being really nice to him so he wouldn't file a restraining order on them. That way they could continue to follow out their plan of filing restraining orders out on him.

It was so sad for me to read these papers. It was just another reminder of how many ways Darvie had been wronged in his short life and, so many times, by the same people.

I had avoided looking over the restraining orders for so long. I just did not have much emotional strength left to look over some things, and I did not want anymore unneeded stress.

Darvis had made an appointment to go talk to the sheriff, and so the private investigator went with him. Darvis wanted to actually talk to the sheriff and see what more could be done on our case. The sheriff didn't even *know* about our case! That was unbelievable to us since the case was twenty eight months old at that time *and* so much had gone on.

When Darvis asked if money was an issue in getting some more things done on the case, the sheriff said that there was plenty of money if we needed to do more. He said that the detective could even start questioning the same people over if needed.

I wanted the Tuolumne County Sheriff's Office to give me permission, so that I could be the one to take the bones that I had found on that property down personally and give it to the forensic doctor myself.

Darvis told the sheriff what I had found and that I did not want to release them. He told him I wanted to be able to take it down myself. The sheriff's office would not allow that and instead wanted me to turn them over to them.

Reluctantly within a few days, I released what I found to them. I had to trust that they really would think it may be something and take it down for me.

It wasn't long until we found out they were just animal bones. I also called the forensic doctor and she confirmed it.

Unbeknownst to us, the sheriff's office had also taken down the small bone fragments that had been found near the water's edge on the property near where our son's remains had been found. She was very kind as she also confirmed to me all the different pieces of bone that she had checked out of our son's remains. I had to try to hold my breath as my ears and mind and then my heart had to take it all in. Listening to the things that she was describing just about did me in.

Father God, what in the world happened to our son!

28

Darvis and I then went with the private investigator to talk with a girl named Megan. Gloria told me exactly where she was living.

I had been looking for Megan for quite a while because I previously heard from Anita, who had contacted me one time before and was now avoiding me, that Darvie and Megan had been together a few days before Darvie went missing.

Unfortunately Megan did not give us much information.

However, she said she felt like some people in Oregon, were behind his disappearance, somehow. She just didn't know exactly how.

One day, I called the private investigator to talk to him about some things that I was thinking about. I couldn't get over the fact that he was just helping us out at no cost to us at the time.

During our conversation, I asked him, "Why are you helping us?"

He said, "My wife and I read your article that was in the newspaper. It just touched both of our hearts, and we just knew that we wanted to help."

Knowing we would have to come up with the money, I asked him also how much it would cost if we were ever able to have him go to Oregon for us.

He said that he would have to let us know.

The private investigator even went to talk to Louie at his place of work, but Louie swore at him and told him that he did not have to talk to him. With that said, Louie just walked away.

The private investigator also went to Chuck the landowner's home to try to talk to him. Even though we had only been to Chuck's home that one time so long ago, Chuck told him that he felt like he was being harassed. The private investigator got nothing out of him either.

After talking to the private investigator though he agreed like I did that Chuck wasn't telling all he knew. That he was definitely hiding something.

It was so frustrating to hear such things, but yet knowing others felt like I did gave me strength somehow to continue my investigating.

Darvis and I went again to talk to the sheriff. I had never been able to go meet with him before, and so I looked forward to seeing what the sheriff had to say.

I told him that I questioned the landowner's innocence, and that if all of the '*druggies*' were taken out of the equation and the landowner had admitted to doing what he did, and then remains were found on his property, the landowner would have been arrested.

The sheriff told me he also did not believe a whole lot in lie detector tests.

It was on this day that Darvis mentioned the crowbar to the sheriff and how we wanted it checked out even more for fingerprints and possibly other evidence.

We walked away without really feeling much hope at all because too much time had passed for law enforcement to be motivated to do much more.

We just didn't know what could be done to find out more truth.

Relying on the Lord, I trusted that everything that came upon me though had filtered through his hands first. I believed that every time a new thought came my way to turn another stone over, that he was the one behind it. I did whatever it took to turn the next stone, no matter how heavy the task was going to be.

29

Finally, we got the long awaited call from Detective Bob. He told Darvis he had been contacted by the guys who would give the lie detector test to Chuck. They were coming to California and asked the detective to get everything ready.

The detective said he had talked to Louie and *once again* Louie agreed to take the test.

I was overjoyed! God was coming through for us again.

We waited with anticipation.

Within a week the detective finally called us to say Louie and Chuck were going to go get their lie detector tests taken within the next couple of days.

He said Louie was going to take his lie detector test first. The test was going to take place in a town about an hour away, the very next day. Chuck's test was going to be the day after that.

I felt so much anxiety about Louie going down to take his test. I couldn't believe the detective was going to actually rely on Louie to be taken down by a friend. The detective talked to Louie's friend and believed they would really show up the next day to take the test.

I did not understand why the detective would not have taken Louie down himself to at least be assured that Louie would really show up. It would have given the detective plenty of time to talk with Louie, and, maybe, just maybe, he would have been able to convince Louie to come forward with the truth.

Yet he didn't. He said he would just meet Louie down there.

During the next day we heard nothing. I figured no news is good news. I knew we would have heard from the detective earlier *if* Louie was a no show *again*.

By early evening, the detective called us to let us know that Louie had indeed showed up. We found out later Louie had completely failed the test.

30

Knowing Louie failed his lie detector test did not come as a surprise to any of us.

It was public knowledge that when people are trying to mess up the lie detector test as they are being questioned, they will bite their tongue or lip or pinch themselves.

Louie knew the tricks of the trade.

We already felt like he knew exactly what happened to Darvie even if he wasn't directly involved.

We heard that he just did not want to be known as a snitch.

The next day we were anxiously waiting to hear back from the detective to see how the lie detector test went with Chuck.

When early evening arrived and the detective finally called Darvis, it was such a big letdown to us to hear him say that Chuck had passed his lie detector test. In fact, the detective said he passed it with flying colors.

The detective said he felt like Chuck did care somewhat about what had happened to us. He said Chuck was maybe just an unusual kind of person and had a weird way of showing he cared.

I was devastated! I just couldn't believe it.

No matter what we were being told, I just knew in my heart Chuck knew something he wasn't telling us.

I mentioned a couple of times something to the detective that I felt was so very important. I asked him that before Chuck took the lie detector test, if someone, somehow in their questioning would please work it out so they could find out something for me.

I wanted to know just exactly how Chuck got the cut on his forehead that he had right after Darvie went missing.

I realized that they never even asked him about the cut. I was so discouraged.

In fact, it wasn't until months later I found out something that just did not sound right.

Although we knew Louie had to go out of town to get his lie detector test taken, I did not know that the next day when Chuck had his lie detector test taken, he was able to have it taken in town locally.

Chuck was never made to go out of town after all.

I was so confused by the sheriff's office's actions...the person they thought was possibly one of the guilty ones was made to go out of town to have their lie detector test done. To me, to make Louie go out of town at least doubled the chances that a test may not have even been taken at all.

Yet the one person that still seemed so suspicious to us, if not necessarily to the sheriff's office had all the accommodations given to them.

I kept wondering if Chuck actually had a *real* lie detector test, or did he just sit down and was questioned? Was Chuck told that they really didn't feel like he was the guilty one, but they just had to do this to appease our family? Why would Chuck not have to go out of town, and Louie, who was the most hardest to get to go in, have to?

It wasn't that I didn't trust Detective Bob because I did. I just thought it did not make any sense to me. I really did not know who all was involved in getting the lie detector tests done anyway. I knew that the sheriff's office did not think the way we did about it.

I questioned the sheriff's office about it months later because I couldn't get it off my mind.

I wanted them to check if he really had taken a *real* lie detector test.

When I had mentioned this to a detective in charge of the Detective Division named Wallace, he wasn't overly friendly to me. He told me Detective Bob had done an excellent job, and I agreed.

When I started telling him about some new things that were being said on the street, without him knowing that I knew what the sheriff had told us about questioning the same people again if needed, he said to me, "Well if you think that we are going to question the same people again, that is not going to happen. We don't have the manpower to do it anyway."

I couldn't believe it.

A new detective by the name of Cooper had just come on board because Detective Bob was soon to be retiring. The sheriff's office wanted someone else to take our case over.

Cooper thought I wanted to see the actual questions that were asked to Chuck during the test so that we could go over them. But that was not what I had asked for.

When Cooper finally got back to me, I was let down again.

I was told, "Yes, it was an actual lie detector test and no, you cannot see it."

31

Approximately, two years after Darvie went missing, a particular situation came my way that will stay with me for the rest of my life.

Shortly after the lie detector tests were given, I received an e-mail from a friend of mine. He was letting me know of another horrible scenario involving Louie that someone he knew just recently told him.

Reading it was almost too much for me to bear.

I couldn't contact my friend fast enough. He gave me the phone number of the man who told him this new scenario.

I had never met this person before that I was about to call, but I did know that this person considered Louie to be a good friend of his. I was anxious to make the call and so I contacted him right away.

The man did seem to care about my loss.

He began to tell me a story that he said someone had told him about what had happened to Darvie. He said the person was speaking firsthand about it, telling him that they had been at the scene of the crime.

When he told me these things, he was being very careful to not mention exactly who it was he had been talking to.

Again, I had to distance myself from this conversation at times. I could not hear such horrible things being said and acknowledge that it was my dear sweet son that was being talked about in this way.

As horrible as the scenarios I had heard about in the past were, this was even more horrific. How could I listen to these things and ever be the same? If this story was true, how could man even *think* to do such things to his own species?

I brought up Louie's name to the man letting him know that Louie had failed his lie detector test. I told him we believed Louie was behind it all somehow. He then said to me that the things he had just told me were told to him by Louie.

I told him, "I am going to continue to investigate no matter what it takes until I find out who is really responsible for what happened to my son."

He told me, "Well, I know that people don't really like you snooping around asking a bunch of questions. You should watch out so nothing happens to you. I'm sure your husband wouldn't want to lose a wife."

As much of a threat as that sounded, the way he said it to me really wasn't like he was threatening me at all.

It made me think someone must have said those things to him regarding me.

I still didn't care what anyone said about my investigating. I was on a mission for the truth, and no one was going to stop me.

I told him, "Well I think that the druggies are a bunch of liars, and I think my son is buried out somewhere on the land out there."

I could tell that he was still listening to what I was saying even though he had heard certain things from Louie.

He told me, "Let me make a few phone calls, and I will get back to you."

Within a half hour I couldn't have received a stranger phone call.

The guy called me back and said before he quickly ended our call, "I think you do need to go back out on that property and make sure you bring those search dogs."

I couldn't believe it!

Was my mother's intuition on to something?

I waited to tell the detective about the phone call because I felt like no one seemed to listen to me, and I was also trying to protect someone.

There were some things that I really believed in that should have been looked at. I felt like law enforcement just brushed them off. I also felt like I had to wait to tell the detective because when I talked with the man, he had wondered if Louie had told *only him* that story. That maybe Louie was waiting to see if he was a snitch. I did not want something to happen to anyone else.

I was waiting to see if anyone, anywhere, would ever tell me the same story so I would know that Louie had again ran his mouth to someone else. I still didn't know if the story was even true or not.

In time, people I encountered on the street began to tell the same story to me with Louie's name again mentioned.

The moment I heard it from someone else, I went straight to the detective to try to convince him to have it looked into.

I showed him the e-mail I had received, but the detective just acted like he didn't believe the story. I could tell that he had no interest in pursuing it.

For whatever reason, nothing was ever done about it at the time.

32

I was so tired of waiting to see when the local law enforcement would get the HRD team out again.

It had already been 19 months since they first searched.

I could not believe that much time had already passed by.

We just kept waiting like the sheriff's office told us to do.

Someone would soon come forward, they said.

Darvis and I continued though to search on our own the whole time along with Kristie and Bobby when they were able to.

We looked in hollow tree trunks and dug in shallow holes. It was so overwhelming.

One particular day when Darvis and I were searching, for whatever reason, all I kept saying from God's word was, *'Not by might nor by power, but by my Spirit,' says the Lord Almighty.*

We eventually knew we just couldn't continue to search on our own anymore.

I finally contacted the HRD team myself and asked them if they would come out again. We really wanted their dogs to search around where our son's remains were found to see if they would *pick up* on anything. They agreed to come out. However they said the sheriff's office would again have to approve it for them to actually come out.

I was suddenly filled with so much anxiety as they mentioned they wanted to have the landowner's permission first to go out. I couldn't believe it! I told them I did not even know if he was innocent or not and I did not see why we had to ask him for anything. I didn't want him to know what we were doing since I did not trust him.

One thing I have never understood is why the Tuolumne County Sheriff's Office never called the property a *crime scene*. I always felt like they should have *made* Chuck stay off his own property until everything could be searched and investigated.

When the search team notified the sheriff's office, unfortunately, Wallace, the same detective that I had talked to before was going to handle that issue. He said he also wanted to talk to Chuck first. He wanted to get Chuck's permission for us all to go on his property.

I just did not understand why so many times it seemed that our local law enforcement acted like they were on the property owner's side and not ours when we really needed them to be fighting for our rights.

Chuck had said in the past that he was tired of people stealing things off of his property even though we never had.

So even though Chuck knew that it was only going to be the search dog team, local law enforcement, myself, and Darvis, he still did not give us permission to go on his property.

With Chuck not giving any of us permission to go on his property, was not that a red flag that the sheriff's office could see? I was devastated when Darvis called to pass the news on to me to say we were not going to be allowed to have another search.

As if we would even want anything materialistic that was on Chuck's property! Darvis said he wouldn't give Chuck $5.00 for everything that was on his property. That is how much invaluable old junk we felt was out there.

I was shocked and in disbelief. I felt like we had been knocked down again.

Though I knew that God was on our side, I still could not understand why this was happening to us.

I stopped everything that I was doing, prayed, and asked him to please help us out with the situation at hand.

Within just a short time, Darvis called me again and said the sheriff's office decided they could make a way for us to still have a search, but the problem was we would not be allowed to go on Chuck's property.

Where our son's remains were found was near the water's edge, which is on a county easement. We could end up on that part of the land, but we would be forced to go around Chuck's property to get down to where we needed to be.

I cried so hard because I was so thankful that the Lord had again provided an open door for us.

I was still thinking what if Darvie was on Chuck's property? Did Chuck know that he was?

No one knew that land more than Chuck did.

So on June 1, 2012, Darvis and I, the HRD team, and the private investigator met up at the top of the road above the property to go on a search.

The local coroner had come representing the sheriff's office. He was going to wait in his vehicle at the top of the road.

We all started out at the top of the road and just began going down the mountain. We were to the left of Chuck's property this time. We split up into two groups. One group consisting of three people, including the private investigator and one dog, went down one way more to the left of us, and Darvis and I went down another way with two other people and another dog, straight down.

The wooded brush has always been so thick. With our heavy boots on and our flannel long sleeve shirts, we constantly were pushing down branches, stepping on and over brush. We had to hold onto manzanita limbs as we made our way down the side of the mountain. Poison oak was everywhere. It could not be avoided.

No matter what we encountered, Darvis and I, would allow nothing to stop us from getting down to the bottom.

Unintentionally Darvis and I split up from our group. I kept getting ahead of myself and Darvis had to continually tell me to slow down. I knew his back and legs were always hurting him, and he had a much harder time than I getting down, but I felt so much in a hurry. I just wanted to hurry and find our son.

As we eventually got down closer to the water's edge, there were so many blackberry bushes. We had to go right alongside the water's edge and even in the water stepping carefully on rocks so we would not slip.

I actually went over to a fallen log in the river, and I did slip and fall. I was just in time to see a snake and watch it slither away into the water. I picked up old torn tarps and any pieces of articles of clothing that I found.

Any item we saw that was out of the ordinary, we explored to see exactly what it was.

When we got closer to our destination, Darvis and I waited for the other two people in our group and their dog to finally reach us. The other group had gotten even more away from our destination by traveling further to the left of us.

Since Chuck had not allowed us to go on his property, everywhere we traveled was even more unfamiliar territory.

This search should have only taken us thirty minutes to get to where we needed to be. If we would have arrived to our destination a lot sooner, we would have had more time to explore in the right areas.

Instead, it ended up taking us two and a half hours to get down to it.

Two and a half hours!

All because *someone* in the sheriff's office thought we needed to ask Chuck if we could go on his property—only for us to be turned down.

Our group eventually arrived at the location we were seeking and we explored the area for awhile.

It was a day of so much time wasted for no reason. The dogs always worked best together, and yet they never did get together. It made the end of the day so discouraging.

When our group decided to start heading back up the mountain, Darvis and I went our own way back up to the top of the road and our search dog team group went another way.

When they arrived at the top, we were there waiting for them.

They said their dog had acted strange around a rodent hole in the ravine but the dog gave them no other signs.

Within a short while, the private investigator found his way up to the top of the road where we were gathered. The other group actually got lost for awhile down below and one of the women had cramping in her legs so badly that they almost had to call for someone to come get her out of the canyon. It was a very discouraging day.

So many people had given their time to help us out, and nothing really had been gained by all that was done that day.

What we did not know was that this would be the last time the private investigator would give his services to us. It seemed all he wanted to do was get out of there. The private investigator left shortly after he made it up to the top. He said he had a prior commitment he had to be at.

Six weeks would go by without any word from him.

I guess I had just been waiting to hear back from him, and, before I knew it, a lot of time had passed by.

Darvis and I decided I would give him a call to see what was up. When I did, he let me know he now had more availability but he would have to charge us if he was to do anymore on our case.

As much as I appreciated his help, I still was surprised it had ended as it did.

After that disappointing search, there was another period of about a year where I did a whole bunch of investigating on my own.

I would begin to seek out people I had wanted to talk to just to see what they knew or what they had heard.

Little did I know it would take me down a really long road with not much help along the way.

33

As I have done during all my investigating, I always have written down people's names I wanted to find or things I wanted to do. As I did them, I have checked them off my list.

I really believe the Lord helped me to think up the things on my list. I would leave no stone unturned. If what I wanted to do was a possibility, I would do it when I felt like the time was right.

If I was to question someone and they lied to me, I always felt if they could look at the mother straight in the eye and lie to my face, well, they would have to live with themselves because I did what I had to do.

I asked someone for help and believed they could be trusted. It was on them if they couldn't be.

There were days where I would take emotional breaks for awhile. Then I would get up and go again and see what I could find out.

Gloria has taken me to so many places. I would never have been able to know where to go if it wasn't for her help. She has known many of the people I have wanted to talk with.

Many of the people I have spoken with I have never met before, but my son did. I have talked to employers of people that I have suspected knew something.

I have met people for lunch to hear what they had to say. I have showed up at people's homes and asked them to please come out and talk with me.

I have called strangers who don't even know who I am.

I have heard so many people's opinions of what they think happened to my son and knowing at the time they were just speculating. They did not know anything.

I have called numbers that Darvie had wrote down and left in his room, hoping the person on the other end could give me some piece of information I did not have.

I have heard unspeakable things.

I have talked with people that have mentioned something to someone, but then once they get confronted by me asking them more questions, their stories always change.

I have talked with people that others have told me are crazy, and that they wouldn't know anything. I have always wondered though if maybe it was them who really did know something. People just think no one will believe a crazy person. But I might…

I have found people that I have talked to in the past and they have told me that they would call me back but never did, to confront them on the questions I still needed answered.

I have called relatives of people that are still in their drug addiction to ask if their family member have ever mentioned anything. If they haven't, I have asked them to please ask them what they have heard.

I would always say to someone to ask their friends and acquaintances, "What do you think happened to Darvis Lee Jr?"

My son was 'one of them' so to speak. He was like a 'brother', to many of them and so knowing there are people here who don't come forward with the truth just breaks my heart. So many people are afraid of losing their drug connection, of all things.

I finally got in contact with Pam that I had encountered on the street that day. God in his perfect timing opened the door for us to meet up again after I tried to locate her for so long. She seemed to want to help me at the time.

She said she did not even remember talking with me before and she had no idea why she sent me to go talk with Kara and Paul. That was very discouraging to hear since the memory of our first encounter has never left my sight.

She tried to get whatever information she could out in the homeless camps around our area, and, for a short while, there were some new names being brought up, one name in particular, Andrew.

Even Karen, Tim's girlfriend, was brought up, as being a part of Darvie's disappearance. I didn't know Karen and the story she previously told law enforcement had not been proven, so I didn't know what to believe.

Even someone out of state who didn't even know Pam started mentioning to me Andrew's name.

I thought that we may really be on to something this time. It was something we had never suspected.

I tried to check out these people, and I started going off thinking in another direction for a few weeks. When I realized the madness it was bringing my way, I knew that I needed to stop, at least for awhile.

Andrew may have just been trying to intimidate people by saying things. I have found that sometimes there are people who just want to feel powerful, but they may know nothing.

I just had to let some things go.

One thing that Pam did tell me eventually is the place where Maria was staying at now. Maria was the woman who had lived at the house where Mark had left his truck. She was also part of the first scenario that Linda had told me and Darvis. I wanted to talk with her and see what she had to say.

First I had to check out something else.

In doing my own investigating, I have been in many different situations that often have been uncomfortable or even not the safest, but I have done it all in my quest to find out the truth about my son.

I have been where angels haven't trod…

One situation in particular stands out that when I look back, all I can say is it probably wasn't such a good idea for me to have done it alone. I was completely out of my element.

It was a time when I had called over at Gloria's house, and asked her to take me to someone's home who lived in the same neighborhood as Debby. Tim, who had told that first scenario to Linda, was staying there. Of course, I wouldn't know any of the people at this house, and I had never met Tim before so I was surprised when I saw that Gloria put a hammer in her back pocket just in case we needed it for protection. Gloria wasn't messing around. She was going prepared.

One of the things that I do that probably drives my husband crazy is that I never involve him when I am going off investigating. A lot of times, I don't let him know what I am doing or where I am going. I don't want him to worry, as I worry how he would handle some of the things that I encounter. Again, I have my family to think about. So I do it for a kind of protection, but it isn't always wise, like in this situation.

God might have made this happen for my protection because Darvis had actually called me once we got over to the house. He was asking me where I was, and I told him I was with Gloria, and I quickly hung up.

A short time later, I accidentally called him from my phone still in my pocket. He heard some of the conversation but couldn't make out most of it. I was not aware of the call I had made.

When we arrived at this house, I saw at least four men and one woman. I could tell right away that almost everybody seemed to be under the influence.

Gloria quickly let Tim know who I was and that I wanted to talk with him. A big metal side of a garage door was lifted up for me and Gloria to enter in the garage. A six-foot long two-by-four held the door up when opened, and was let down as soon as we were in.

For a moment, I thought how it was just us three inside there, and I wouldn't know how to get out if I wanted to. One section of the big garage was made out to be someone's bedroom.

As soon as I stepped into the bedroom, I noticed a hangman's noose dangling from the ceiling right above the bed. Just for a second, I felt a chill run down my whole body, and, inside, I felt fear thinking how Gloria and I could be overtaken by someone, but it only lasted for a few seconds. I was so out of my comfort zone.

I turned my focus on what I had come for. I asked Tim his thoughts on what happened to my son.

He really wasn't giving me any straight answers, but, as soon as I mentioned Louie's name, his whole disposition changed. It was like he closed up inside and our talk was pretty much done. He basically said he didn't know anything.

He looked at Gloria and reminded her that it was only because I was Darvie's mom that he was even talking with me at all. If I was anyone else, he wouldn't have.

Looking back now, I can't believe the same thing happened here like it did when Darvis and I had talked with Louie. I had completely forgotten to mention to Tim about what I had heard that he had told people.

He gave me no answers.

The last thing he said as he looked at Gloria as we were leaving was, "This never happened. You were never here."

34

By the time we got out to the driveway, Gloria had pulled another man out with us and asked him to tell us what he had heard. He told us about a scenario at a house that wasn't even in the neighborhood. That was the first time that I had ever heard about that particular house before.

What was strange was that the house he was talking about was Maria's mom's house. It was the same house where Maria would eventually tell me she had been staying, supposedly when Darvie went missing.

The scenario was the same as we had heard from Linda that involved Mark but this man added another part to it that was almost too much for me to listen to.

Oh, how I prayed he was wrong.

It still brought new thoughts my way, and I started thinking that maybe the dogs should go to Maria's mom's house too.

It wasn't long before I had convinced myself this was another case of somebody saying something that someone had told someone else. I was so sick of secondhand news.

Detective Bob was now getting ready to actually retire. I just didn't know what we were going to do once he was off the case. Our biggest supporter from our local law enforcement would soon be gone.

He came over to our house one night and at first Darvis and him talked awhile.

They always knew they had better get *all* that they had to say out first, because I always had *a lot* to say.

Detective Bob was trying to tell us how he thought Mark was the sole person responsible for Darvie's death, and that he felt Mark had acted alone.

He told us that the remains that we found of our son could not have been a more important find. He said it was like God's way, of letting our family know at least Darvie was not with us any longer, so we could have some closure.

He said we knew Darvie was not suffering anymore, and that he was with the Lord and that one day true justice would be served.

He told me how he worried about me, like I was allowing this to run my life too much.

He said Darvie wouldn't want me to keep searching and not have any peace in my life.

He didn't want to see me give up living when I had a whole lot of wonderful family members that loved me and still needed me.

When I interjected quickly and mentioned offering a bigger reward of $50,000, Detective Bob said there was no reason to put our reward higher.

He said if someone else had really known what had actually happened, they would have already come forward for the reward, no matter how much it was.

Darvis had a different mindset than I had. He felt like when God wanted us to know the truth, if we really *needed* to know it, the Lord would bring it basically right in our laps.

I think this has helped my husband to be able to deal with his pain.

Being a man, he wanted to *fix* this situation. And because it seems to not be getting *fixed* the way he wants it to, he can not dwell on it in the way that I choose to do.

Now it was my turn to speak.

I said I disagreed about the reward. I told the detective that if we put the reward to $50,000 and no one came forward with what we were wanting, then we would never have to pay it. But if someone did come forward, it would be well worth paying out the $50,000.

I said I knew the previous reward amounts were a lot of money but maybe, just maybe, $50,000 might just make someone come forward and take us straight to the truth.

I felt like it wouldn't hurt anything to increase the amount.

In the past, many people have told me if someone would just come forward with the truth, even $10,000 could at least have given someone enough money to protect themselves and move away and start a new life somewhere else.

We have never really publicized having a reward for a long time now. However, I intend to remind the media after my story gets out.

I told Detective Bob that because he was not with me all the time, he did not know that my faith was even stronger. It had never wavered. I told him I had people that had told me they were encouraged by my strength and my faith. I told him that I do a lot of things besides my investigating.

I said believing that Mark acted alone, would never be something I could believe. I also told him I did not know of the landowner's innocence anyway.

I told him as I tried to hold back the tears that fought their way out, "I appreciate everything that you have done for us, but if all *you* found was the jawbone of your son, that would *never* be enough, and as far as Darvie not wanting me to keep searching, absolutely he would."

I knew my son, and he definitely wanted me to do as I was doing.

I said our son's blood was crying out for justice.

35

Since I now knew where Maria was staying, I made plans with Gloria to go with me so I could talk with her. It was obvious Maria had been friends with Mark and also with Louie. With Mark's truck parked at her house when he was arrested, I figured she may be able to tell me something. I knew she had children so I had already planned that if I had to I was going to *beg* her *mother to mother* to please tell me what she knew.

We found Maria in a little travel trailer. She said she had just arrived home.

I loved seeing how God did things like that, preparing the way for me to talk with people.

I asked her lots of questions, but it did not take long for me to see, she had been tight with Mark, Louie, and even Andrew.

I told her I wanted people to know that I was still coming around, and I was not going to stop until I got my answers.

I mentioned to her the scenario with her in it that I had heard. She was adamant that nothing had ever happened to anyone while she was at home. She said that she only knew Darvie because he had given her a ride one time, a long time ago, and that was all.

She said she knew nothing, and that she would even take a lie detector test if needed. She said with no disrespect to me, she thought that it would be *neat* to take one.

I was thinking that there would be no reason for us to check out her old house and to bring the search dogs there if she hadn't been there like we had been told, when she suddenly said, "But what would it hurt to bring the dogs out?"

With that statement, I looked at Maria and wondered if she was telling me something, without telling me directly.

All along I have always put her with the scenario that I had heard in the past, thinking she was living there at the time. When she told me that she had moved out by the time Darvie had went missing and had been living with her mom and I could verify it by talking to her mom, it dawned on me that maybe she *wasn't* there. Maybe she *had* moved out.

It could have been vacant at the time, and something could have still happened there.

However, at this time, Louie was still living at her old house.

How could I get the HRD team to search her old place if Louie was still there?

I wasn't about to let my husband know.

I would just have to wait until I knew Louie moved.

People came and went in those homes.

It was only a matter of time.

Gloria and I left, and both of us agreed that we believed her. We believed that she knew nothing.

It wasn't long until old acquaintances of Maria told me, "Don't believe a word Maria ever says".

A lie detector test in Maria's future may be something we may need to take place eventually.

Would any of this ever get any easier?

Then something strange happened that made me think that we were on to something again.

I told Darvis that we had never searched the end of the road away from the landowner's property.

Since we really didn't know what happened, we always stayed at a certain area, but how did we know our son's remains weren't over there?

I also started thinking about the burn pile on the helicopter pad. I asked Gloria if she would ever come with me and help me dig if I brought some shovels. Of course she said she would.

Darvis and I had never spoken to anyone about the helicopter pad, and no one else had ever mentioned it to us.

It wasn't long after though, that I got connected to a woman named Tina through an acquaintance of mine.

She seemed more than willing to help me out, and she told me everything that she had ever heard.

I was shocked when she told me that she had heard that something had happened at Maria's house, but that there was a burn pile on an airplane pad where things had been buried.

Did she just say an airplane pad? Did she mean the helicopter pad?

I could not believe someone had mentioned the helicopter pad to me when we had never told anyone else on the street about it.

Tina said she would try to find out more.

The next time I talked with Tina, she said she had asked her cousin what he knew. She made sure that he did not know she had been talking to me.

He mentioned Maria's house and the helicopter pad also. He also mentioned an end of a road up a very steep mountain to a clearing.

It was the end of the road past the landowner's property, just as I had been thinking.

Come to find out, Tina's cousin happened to be Tim. The guy who had been at that place Gloria and I should have never gone to.

A few days later when Tina asked Tim some more questions, he realized that she had been talking to me and then he gave no more answers.

Tina said when she brought up Louie's name to Tim he had nothing nice to say about Louie. Tina said in fact it really upset Tim to hear Louie's name being mentioned at all.

Even though Tim had actually considered Darvie a friend, it was obvious he still did not want to get involved.

I was thrilled to get some hope again that maybe soon we would finally find the truth of what had happened to our son.

Then I found out Louie had finally moved out of Maria's old house.

I saw God's hand in this for sure.

I was now ready to make my move.

We just had to get the HRD team out there again. This time I had five different places I was going to ask the search dog team to stop the dogs by and let them run around at.

Two out of the five would only take a few minutes.

I would have to contact them again and see if they would be willing one last time to come out. I knew this would be our last shot with the sheriff's office.

I sent the e-mail to the HRD team on May 14, 2013.

I explained to them the places of interest I was concerned about.

I told them I knew it was our last shot.

When I heard back from them, they said they were willing to go out again.

They wanted me to contact the sheriff's office and see if they would agree to another search. If they agreed, then I would get back to the search dog team so that we could try and set a date.

It all fell into place.

June 14, 2013 would be the day we would go out again.

36

Before the search date was set, Cooper had completely taken over our case, and he came over to our house to talk with us.

He basically told us the same things that Detective Bob had said.

He too felt Mark was the sole person responsible for Darvie's death, and that he had acted alone.

It was like if we agreed, maybe the case could be closed.

Not a chance.

I told him, I would never believe that.

During our visit I expressed to Cooper that I had five places that I would like checked out if we were able to go out on a search.

I had high hopes when he first showed up thinking maybe, just maybe, we would all be on the same page for once.

We were hoping for a detective that would see our son's case with new eyes and possibly start looking in a different direction.

Darvis and I were sure bummed out when he left.

It wasn't long after his visit, that Cooper called and said he would like to meet with me and Darvis again at the sheriff's office.

This time, McDonald, the Sergeant, was present as well, and Cooper asked what five things on a search I wanted them to do and why.

I could understand him asking me, and I was particularly pleased to see him with a notepad and pen. For quite a while now, every time Darvis and I or even me by myself came in and had a lot of information to talk about, no one seemed to ever take notes anymore. It always made me feel so frustrated because even though I had my own notes, I wondered how they would ever remember *all* the things I asked them to do.

As I spoke, he wrote.

Regarding each location, I explained in detail my reasons for wanting them checked out.

I also let them know I knew it was our last shot.

The five locations I was concerned about and wanted searched were:

1. Maria's old home in Debby's neighborhood.
   It is the same place where Mark's truck had been found.
2. A place called *The Switchback*.
   It was on the same road that took us eventually to the property where we had been searching. It was over an embankment off the side of the road.
3. A place over a hillside where we on one of our searches had found a whole bunch of animal bones scattered.
4. A burn pile on a helicopter pad where the search dogs had already searched before but I was getting more new tips recently.
5. The end of a road over a creek and up a steep dirt road to a big clearing.

When I was done mentioning the five locations and explaining the importance of why I wanted to have them checked out, Cooper said they would have to get back to us.

Even though Cooper was now handling our case, it was evident right away that he had his opinion, and I had mine. He let me know with an attitude that things just didn't set right between us from the very beginning, that it was definitely *my* opinion and not *his*.

How I prayed that the Tuolumne County Sheriff's Office would give us one last shot.

It was less than two weeks later, that we arrived in the early morning hours at an agreed upon location. It was the morning of our search.

37

The night before our search I asked the Lord to please help us to find *something*.

I did not think I was asking too much from him.

I had always been told that if you search for the truth long enough, eventually you will find it.

I just had to believe that.

I felt like my son's remains were in the vicinity of where we were going to search.

I just wanted him found.

The HRD team and the sheriff's office wanted to start our search at the last place I had mentioned, which was at the end of a road over a creek and up a steep dirt road to a big clearing.

The more I thought about it, no matter how anxious I was to go to the other places, that location did seem like the most probable place to start, really.

The anxiety I was feeling the night before we went out on our search wasn't anything new.

I was always anxious each time we were about to go out to search for our son's remains.

By morning I always started out with new hope.
I knew I had to trust the Lord.
This time especially...
All I kept saying was "*The appointed time is now!*"

38

I was surprised to see Sergeant McDonald was the one that showed up the morning of our search and not Cooper, the detective that was supposedly handling our case.

I told McDonald earlier after our meeting at the sheriff's office without any disrespect meant, that I knew way more about our case than a new detective coming in. I felt like I should have had more respect shown to me. McDonald agreed.

Having McDonald on board with us has proven to be a Godsend for sure though.

There were four vehicles this time including our own.

Plans were changed on our way up to search that morning when the HRD team figured since it was on our way, we would stop over at the helicopter pad first.

The same dogs had already combed that area a few weeks after Darvie had gone missing. This time I was hoping that they would spend more time checking it out.

Darvis and I had driven up to this site a couple of weeks earlier, and our truck had actually gotten stuck from us trying to drive up to the pad.

We tried to use the shovels that we had brought to get us unstuck, however the dirt was too compacted down and we couldn't even dig our truck out of it.

While our truck was stuck, we decided to just walk up to the pad and see if we could dig at the burn pile. However, we couldn't even dig a cup full of dirt. I quickly lost all enthusiasm.

Darvis said he just didn't think there could be anything under the burn pile because it was so compacted down. I said anything was possible...

I asked Darvis, if one day in the future, if I wanted him to, would he bring a backhoe up to the site. He said of course he would.

After realizing that the ground was too hard to dig, we soon had to figure out how to get our truck out.

We were really in a pretty secluded area with hardly any cell service available, but we prayed, and shortly after we prayed, a man came driving by in a truck and had just what we needed to pull us out. Come to find out, he had gone to school with Darvie.

Now being back here with the HRD team again, we didn't stay very long at this location. We were told that the dogs just didn't *pick up* on anything, even when they were around the burn pile.

The steep terrain over the edge just doesn't make it possible for the dogs, let alone humans to try to climb down it and look around.

I had to let it go at this time. I had to trust God. I knew he could make anything happen. I knew he knew what was best for us and that he wanted the truth to come out just as much as we did, but maybe this just wasn't the spot.

I had to be okay walking away from this site, for the time being…

Next we drove a short ways and stopped at the hillside where we knew all those animal bones were. Only one of the dogs went down this time. A short time later when they came back up, we were told the dog just didn't respond to anything. They also said that they never found any of the animal bones that we had previously seen.

Darvis and I had recently came back here to this location, but the brush was so much thicker than it was originally, which was again so discouraging.

One day soon I plan on going there again to try to find the animal bones.

I will collect them all and take them down to the sheriff's office to have them checked out.

I had to walk away from this location too. For only a little while…

The long awaited search was next.

We continued down the dirt road for a few miles until it dead-ended at the creek.

We all left our vehicles and started the long hike up the steep winding dirt road.

I had again been to this location only recently. I had brought Tina and Gloria with me and a friend of Tina's. I wanted to come out, look around, and try to see the location that Tim, who was Tina's cousin, had been talking about.

Nothing was found but two snakes were spotted in two different locations.

So coming out again, I knew it was going to be a hot summer day. With our long sleeve flannel shirts and heavy boots on, it was going to be quite the hike.

As the HRD team, Darvis, myself, and McDonald hiked up the road, it was quite a sight to see. The road had so many deep crevices in it as years of runoff had traveled the same path over and over again. Back and forth the deep crevices were. We had to be careful so we wouldn't fall in one.

Even if someone wanted to drive up this road with a four-wheel drive vehicle, it would have been very difficult. None of us would have even attempted it. Mark might have though with his vehicle since we had heard that he was four wheeling in his truck at the time.

As we made our climb up the mountain, many times I would get to a place that was riddled with beer cans, and I would think to myself, maybe here, maybe here...

My husband whose legs had always bothered him kept up with us all even though I knew his legs were hurting him so badly. Nothing could have held him back.

All the hiking I had done on our previous search that had taken us so long to get down the mountain, had caused me to have horrible charley horses in my leg that evening. I was hoping that I would not have to repeat that again, this time.

One of the groups in the HRD team went down the hillside toward the direction of the creek below. They were gone for awhile and when they came back, they said the dog had seemed to have picked up on something. They marked their GPS as they had always done to be able to mark the location if and when they needed to ever go back to it.

Then we all continued to hike up the road as it winded and got steeper the more we climbed.

Every time we thought we were at a clearing, we would glance a little bit further and see that the road continued.

Eventually we all made it up to the top of the mountain.

There it was! A great big clearing!

To the left of us was a road that had a locked gate across it. The road obviously led to a residence somewhere nearby.

To the right of us was a road that continued winding up to an even higher mountain.

We decided to stay at this clearing and have the dogs look around.

We all walked around in different directions. I prayed and prayed that something would be found. I kept thinking when is this nightmare going to end?

McDonald had walked a ways up on the road that continued up the mountain. Darvis had used his cell phone on Google Earth to locate us and he could see even more clearings up that way. It was somewhere else that could be searched in the future if necessary.

When I decided to walk up toward the higher mountain, McDonald met me on my way up and showed me fresh bear tracks. That was pretty scary to me.

Kristie had originally done some research about bears in our area after we had our community search. She found out there are no grizzly bears out in the wild in the state of California any longer.

We had heard from one neighbor though who lived down the road from this actual property, that there definitely are other kinds of bears that he has seen from time to time around here.

We ended up heading back down the mountain on the dirt road, and it wasn't long that we were on the original dirt road we had come up on. One of the dogs started acting strange around a certain area, and they had brought the other dog down there too because they wanted to see if the other dog would pick up on it also.

The HRD team wanted to show us the behavior their dogs were having around a certain tree. It was evident that the dogs were acting different. They were doing a form of "lifting their jaws" and acting like they were "tasting" something.

When they checked with their GPS radios, the HRD team were able to tell that this location and across the dirt road where the other group had gone earlier, coincided with each other. With further checking, they could see that it was also connected way down below where the remains had been found.

By now, it was pretty hot, and the HRD team knew that the dogs were now getting tired. In the heat, scents travel upward and the dogs have a harder time trying to figure out what direction the scents are coming from.

The HRD team narrowed an area up above that was kind of in the shape of a big triangle where the dogs had acted differently.

The HRD team told me the dogs would never act that way if there was not any kind of remains at that location.

Even though I knew that this was our last shot with them all, I was sure pleasantly surprised when the HRD team mentioned coming back again in a few months when it was cooler, and McDonald totally agreed.

God once again opened another door.

We all started our descent down the road. It was a long hard day of searching and we still had two more places I had wanted them to stop at.

The place called *the switchback* and the property where that house was in Debby's neighborhood.

By the time we drove down to the switchback, I had gained a new sense of anticipation.

Maybe here is where something would be found…

We all stayed close to the road while one dog and then the other dog went down and explored with their trainers. This corner of the road had garbage strewn all over the place. Black bags of who knows what, laid in the crevices of the ravine. Old tires had been tossed, and sand was all over one side of the embankment.

Here again Darvis and I, and Gloria and her husband had come before.

Another time it was just Darvis and I.

We had walked down below, and I had wanted so badly to be able to go through every single piece of garbage there and open every single black garbage bag. I wanted to bring a pick and dig my way through the things. However, it wasn't long being down there in all that debris, and one would realize how overwhelming it became *and* that we could have just been sent on another wild goose chase because this too was rumored.

The HRD team combed this area for quite a while. The dogs were just not picking up on anything at all.

I had to again trust the Lord, to be able to walk away and let it go.

Our team finally arrived at the house I had wanted to search. It had a big metal gate at the beginning of the driveway. It appeared that no one was home. There was a big pit bull dog chained up in the driveway. We also heard at least one other dog in the house.

This was the place Darvis and I had been out to a couple of times in our original search that we had done ourselves. It had the horse carcass over the side of the embankment.

A short time after we got there, people who lived on that street started to come out of their homes. Suddenly people were running back and forth to each other's houses. We felt if any drugs were around, they had quickly been flushed down their toilets or hidden.

It was evident we were not welcome there.

I noticed a woman standing by one of the houses nearby. I recognized her as Judy, from the time that she and her husband had gone out with Darvis and I, and they had searched in some mines for us. I called out her name to try to be friendly.

She yelled back that the tenants of the house were not home. She said that the pit bull sometimes slipped its collar.

Someone in the neighborhood had called the tenants wherever they were to tell them that we were there at their house, and the tenants were possibly going to be arriving soon.

The HRD team and the sergeant did not want to risk their dogs' lives by taking the chance of encountering the pit bull. They also did not want to be forced to do anything to the pit bull if all of a sudden it became territorial and escaped its collar as they were walking by.

McDonald said we would have to try to get a search warrant if we were to come back.

Getting a search warrant would have been very difficult. Except for me saying that we needed to go check out the place, I really had no proof of *why* it would be necessary.

I planned on trying to find out who lived there first. Then I would see if I could get them to agree to let us come there to look around.

I had heard of another person that had lived there before, even before Louie had moved in.

I previously sought out that person's relatives to try to get the guy to talk to me since I heard that he possibly knew something, but no one had ever replied back to me as usual.

The HRD team told the neighbors they didn't want to put anyone's animal in danger, but that it would only be a matter of time and we would be back.

I was so bummed out. I guess I always thought that law enforcement could just walk up to a house and tell the residents they were just going to look around outside on their property, no questions asked. Apparently I was wrong. No one can use their power that way.

Even though we had the landlords' written permission to search a*ny* of his property to look for our son's remains, the tenants have rights, and you cannot just go searching through someone's home and property without permission. Law enforcement knew that. I just didn't.

I came harmless, just wanting to look around. I didn't care what anyone was doing in their home. It was not them that I was interested in at the time.

My heart yearned for the truth. I just wanted so badly to find our son's remains.

But how was I going to find out who it was who lived there? I knew that somehow I would eventually find out, but, even after I did, how would I convince them to let us come search out the property?

God works in such mysterious ways.

It wouldn't be long and I would be in awe again.

I would soon be able to see him orchestrating all the details to fall completely together, and he would connect me with the person who indeed lived there.

39

A few months went by, and I knew the time would soon arrive when we would go search on the mountain again. The plan was to go toward the end of October 2013.

Darvis and I were concerned because we were so afraid it would rain or even snow by then, but the HRD team said that rain wouldn't affect their search at all.

I wondered who I could get to come with me as I made plans to go to that house and talk with the person that lived there.

I thought of Gloria and knew she would go with me if I wanted her to. However, I thought of asking a woman from the HRD team who we had worked with for so long. I knew she would probably agree to go with me too. I thought it might have helped for the person to meet her also and show them we meant no harm.

A different turn of events took place to get me where I wanted to be.

These next accounts of what happened may seem trivial to someone else other than myself, but all these things did not take place without God's hand from above.

I had to first know who it was that lived at that house.

I remembered I had met with some people on the same street about a year earlier. I had taken this guy Benny that lived there out to some mines to look inside of them for me. Even though he said he would help me again when the weather got better, I had never heard back from him.

I still had his cell phone number. I texted him and I told him I knew Louie had moved out of the house down the street from him and I was wondering if he could tell me the name of the person that lived there now. He quickly responded and I had the name. Ted.

I happened to be somewhere soon after that, and I saw a man who I knew worked for the landlord of that house. I quickly asked if he knew who was living in that house now. He started acting like he didn't know, until I brought up the name.

Then he conveniently remembered.

For some reason he mentioned where Ted's sister worked.

That was all the information I needed.

I contacted someone I knew that worked at the same place, to see if they knew her. They did and I found out the department and the hours that she would be at work.

Within days I was at her place of work but unfortunately she happened to be off that day. It was the weekend and I would have to wait a couple more days, before I could come back.

That same evening, I called in an order for takeout from a local restaurant and the person who took my order happened to be someone I knew named Molly. I knew Molly also worked another job for the same company that Ted's sister worked at but just in a different town. I couldn't wait to see her and ask if she knew the woman.

When I arrived to pick up my order, I quickly asked Molly. She said that she did not know her. What was so awesome though, was that one of the waitresses *just happened* to be right behind her and heard what I was asking and Molly said, "But she does."

I couldn't believe it.

This chain of events would not have even happened if the waitress had been across the room at the time.

I asked the waitress what she thought about the woman. I wanted to make sure when I contacted her and asked her what kind of guy her brother was, if she thought he would talk with me.

She told me only nice things about the woman, but what I liked was that she also told me that she knew Ted, and told me that he was a nice guy too.

Again, it was all the information that I needed. I did not have to go look up his sister anymore. I had gotten my answer.

Now I still had to figure out who was going to come with me to talk with him. Before I could make that decision, this same weekend when it was getting late in the evening, I happened to have my Facebook site opened up, looked over, and saw that an acquaintance of mine, Louise, was online.

I had contacted her a few months back as I had tried to do with *anybody* and *everybody* that I knew had known Darvie. I wanted to know at that time what she had heard, or if she knew anything. She was supposed to have talked with someone for me, and I had not heard back from her yet.

I quickly private messaged her and asked her to call me. She called me right away. Louise filled me in on what she had heard, but it really wasn't anything new. Then we were just casually talking.

I started to talk about the area where Darvie's car had been found and the neighborhood that we were looking into.

I told Louise how I had heard how the mountain seems to *call* people up to it. She agreed.

She mentioned that in fact she had been up at that mountain that very weekend. I then asked her specifically if it was actually *the* mountain, and she said yes. For some reason I took it farther and asked her if it happened to be in the *same* neighborhood that I was thinking about. She said that it was.

I asked her if she knew anyone that lived on this particular road. She slowly answered yes, and I mentioned some names of people I had heard had lived on that road and asked her if she knew them. She said she did not.

I mentioned a particular house with a gate. She slowly said, "Yes, why?" I mentioned Ted's name to her.

We both could not believe where our conversation was taking us.

She said "Yes, I know him. In fact, I met him just this weekend *and* I was just at *that* house."

I was astonished with the news.

I filled her in on why I was doing so much inquiring. I asked her if she thought he would let me bring the search dogs out to his place. She said he was a nice guy and she thought he would.

I couldn't figure out what our connection was since I would never have put her in the middle of all this. I was not going to ask her to speak for me because I did not want her involved in case I did have to go through the court system to try to get a search warrant. Again she agreed with me.

She said maybe the reason for the connection on this was because it was a way that she was being told by God to get *off* the mountain. This particular area is where the rundown trailers are sporadically spaced throughout one real big mountain where drugs are rampant in many of the area. Louise knew that it wasn't a good place for her to be. I told her she should stay away from there because she deserved so much more.

We finished our conversation and I hung up.

Within ten minutes I got a call back from her and she said, "I just talked to Ted and he said that he would have no problem with you bringing out the search dogs."

40

Seeing how God worked all that out for me was amazing. I was so in awe.

Louise gave me Ted's number and the next day, I was on the phone with him. He told me he had known Darvie and gave me his condolences. He said he understood our family needed closure. I told him how much I appreciated his willingness to help us out. I told him we wanted to come out in about a month, and he said that would be fine. I tentatively gave him a date. I told him I would talk to him again before we came out.

Within a couple of weeks I contacted Ted again and asked if I would be able to meet him before we came out. He said I could.

A few days before our search, I contacted Louise, and I asked her if she could go with me to see Ted. She texted me right back and told me she was actually at his house and I could come over right then if I wanted to.

When I arrived, Louise and Ted both came out for him to meet me. He was very polite. He gave me a hug and his condolences again.

He told me that no one was going to be home on the day of the search, and he would have his dog with him and the other dog would be in the house. I asked him if there was a place where the dogs could go under his house just in case we needed them to search there. He said he would remove some siding if he couldn't find an opening for the dogs to go in.

Ted gave me written permission for us to come on the property. I thanked him and I was on my way.

October 30, 2013

The morning of our search arrived. The plan was to go up to the house first before we went up to the other property.

We met up at our normal meeting place before setting out. The HRD team arrived and McDonald came alone again. An officer in a patrol car also showed up. The officer would go with us to the house while the dogs were combing the area, just to make sure that everything went smoothly.

Darvis and I led the way.

I was very nervous as we were driving there. I just hoped everything would be all right when we arrived. We were going to be showing up at the house a little earlier than planned so it made me more nervous.

When we arrived at the house, we noticed Ted was at home. His dog was inside and the whole time we were there we heard people in the house, but no one came out.

Oh, how I wished something would be found. This house had been the talk of so many rumors.

The dogs worked behind the house and down the embankment. We were there for quite a while.

Knowing there were people in the house, the neighbors' dogs threatening to come over, and a neighbor shouting out aggressively to another stray dog roaming around, just added to the stress I was already feeling. I wanted the dogs to go under the house, check on the other side of the house, etc. but it was not to be. The HRD team said their dogs did not pick up on anything.

I didn't want to waste anyone's time. I appreciated everyone coming out.

I originally wanted to take the dogs inside the house long before this guy had lived there. In time I had come to realize that finding out *where* something happened did not always give the answers we needed.

I just wanted to know where my son's remains were.

Now, I just had to believe his remain's were not here. I knew that something could have happened to my son at this house and then he was taken away. The dogs could never pick up on that. I really did not know if this house was where anything originated at. All I knew was that it ruled out some rumors. Again I had to trust the Lord and move on.

When the dogs were back in the vehicles and everyone was still in the driveway getting ready to leave, I walked back close to the house and shouted out a big 'thank you' through an open window. I so much appreciated that he had given permission for us to search.

After our last search at the other property, Darvis had done some research and found a road we could take that would bring us up to the top of the mountain to the big clearing. By taking this road, we would not have to walk up that treacherous steep dirt road again to arrive at the same destination.

We had to drive further this time to get there, but it was worth going that way in the end. We recently had rain, and so some of the dirt roads that we were on had deep water holes. Darvis and I questioned if everyone would be able to make it with their vehicles, but they did. The officer left after the search at the house, but there were still three vehicles following us.

We stopped at a new clearing, and there was a big burn pile there. I just wanted the dogs to find the answer to all our questions. My heart was so heavy with so much anticipation.

I got out of our car and headed down the road by myself and started to pray. I hadn't walked too far before I remembered the bear print we had seen the last time. I knew it wasn't too far down from where I was at. I decided to linger awhile and wait for the vehicles to catch up with me.

When we all got down to the original clearing where we had searched the last time, the search dog team headed toward the triangle area that the dogs had shown interest in last time. When we all got down there, the dogs were acting up around a fallen old tree trunk. There the dogs found an old wood rats nest.

Search dogs have actually found human bones in wood rats' nest's before. You have to sift through it all. The search team told me that bones found inside of nests are brown in color, but almost immediately as the sunlight touches them, they turn white.

I quickly ran up the hill to help. With a metal bar in my hands, I began to dig in the tree trunk. I sifted with my fingers as gently as I could. I shoveled out the inside debris left inside. I desperately searched for anything that I could find that would tell me we were on the right track.

But nothing was found.

I don't know much of anything else that could be worse than a mother searching for her son in the way that I had just done. I was almost too numb from the experience.

One group from the HRD team wanted to go down across the dirt road to the area where their dog had acted up before. They also wanted to head down in the direction where some of our son's remains had been found.

They needed one of us to go with them and knowing Darvis could not make the hike easily and knowing how I was game for anything, I volunteered.

I had actually gotten charley horses in *both of my legs at the same time* the evening of our previous search when I had hoped that it wouldn't be so. I could almost not handle that pain when it had came upon me so suddenly.

But this time I was trying to keep myself more hydrated so I hopefully would not have to experience that again.

The three of us and the dog started to hike down the mountain. Even though the terrain was so congested, it was still more open at the top of the mountain than any of our previous searches. We still had to push branches out of our way, step over logs, scoot on our rears in certain areas, and crawl on our knees under branches. We went side to side as we descended down. Their GPS would be able to track their dog as it went ahead of us into the thick bushes and trees.

Due to the recent rain, we were able to notice huge bear tracks. I told them, "This is the grandfather of them all."

Thoughts of meeting up with one, kept me on my toes somewhat but with my heavy boots on and the exhaustion that was soon upon me from the hike, I didn't know how I would quickly get back up the steep mountainside if I was ever forced to.

We were gone for quite a while and traveled quite a distance downward about 150 yards. Eventually the dog was in such thick brush that they were not able to see where he was visually, only to track him on the GPS. They were questioning if we should continue down.

I knew it was still such a far way down to the creek below, and I knew it was going to be quite the hike going back up the mountain. They asked me what I thought and I told them I felt like if we were to find anything that day, we would. I said that I was okay going back up.

As we made our way back up the mountain, I had plenty time to think. I knew this really was our last shot with them. The HRD team and the Tuolumne County Sheriff's Office had helped us out tremendously. There just seemed to be nothing else we could do.

But unbeknownst to us, the other group of the HRD team and McDonald had been talking. The other group in the HRD team didn't know why they couldn't go back on Chuck's property because the dogs were acting interested in that direction.

By the time that we arrived back up with them, I saw them both look at each other and the HRD team say, "We just *have* to come back" and McDonald saying, "We just *have* to."

If that wasn't the sweetest words to my ears, hearing the search dog team say, "And you have to bring the forensic dogs" was.

41

The forensic dogs were a part of a HRD team from another county. These dogs are specially trained and certified canines in the field of human remains detection and forensic evidence.

These dogs are strictly cadaver dogs and are less apt to be distracted by animal bones.

It wasn't much over a year ago that dogs like these located several graves of victims whose lives were taken from them over twenty years earlier.

Darvis contacted this forensic dog team at one time and asked them if they would help us out. They were willing but said only if our local sheriff's office requested them.

Darvis had asked Detective Bob several times to contact them for us.

McDonald said he would see if he could first get Chuck's permission for them to come out. Otherwise, he said he would have to try to get a search warrant.

I didn't want him to ask Chuck anything. I didn't trust him knowing what we were doing. and I said as much.

But who I did trust was my Heavenly Father. He again opened another door for us. He always showed me that he cared so much about the desires of my heart. I knew if he did not think something was necessary to lead us to the truth, the doors would never have opened. God knew what would happen to my heart if I would always have to wonder.

One thing I found encouraging, as we were just about to part, was that the HRD team and somewhat McDonald really seemed to be on the same page as we were, as far as the landowner went. They agreed that it made little sense the things that he had done, and that made me feel like they too might be questioning his innocence.

To have others on board with us in the way that we were thinking gave me hope.

The HRD team told me to give the sheriff's office a couple of weeks, and then if I hadn't heard back from them, to give them a call.

I would try to be patient as we waited…

I probably waited about three weeks, and when I didn't hear back from McDonald, I called him and asked what he had found out. He said he was working on getting the search warrant ready to present it to the judge. He had to get everything worded just right so that it wouldn't get kicked back out. I asked him if he was going to let the judge know that we didn't really know about Chuck the landowner's innocence, and how he had not even given us permission to go on his property.

McDonald said he was going to let the judge know all that. I asked him if I should write to the judge myself. He said only if the judge ended up not signing it.

I knew I would have to wait and just be more patient.

Another couple of weeks went by, and then I contacted the HRD team to see if they had heard anything. They said they hadn't so I made another call to McDonald, but I didn't hear back. A week or so went by and I called again. After the third call that I made, I got a hold of him. I asked him how things were going regarding getting the search warrant.

He said he didn't think it would be much longer and when I asked him if he thought the judge would sign it, he said he thought that he would. I asked McDonald about the forensic dogs coming out and if anything was scheduled and he said another person was in charge of that and was getting that all ready. I thanked him and hung up.

Little did I know that within just a couple of hours, the judge would sign the search warrant. Finally, plans would be made to bring the forensic dogs out to search the landowner's property. For the first time, we would not be contacted to be a part of this search. We would not even hear about it until it was over.

42

Within a few days from the time I talked to McDonald, the search was set up and done.

I had heard Chuck did not show up when they were there which was a good thing.

I did not know why Darvis and I were not included on the search this time.

I would assume the forensic search dog team did not think the parents of the victim needed to be present.

I couldn't believe it when McDonald called me and said that within two hours of the last time we talked, he had a signed search warrant. I was disappointed when he told me that just the day before, they all went out on the search. As he started to talk, I just knew in my heart he was going to tell me in the end that they had found nothing. I just wanted to cry.

McDonald said there were three dogs that day and they had combed a big part of the land all day.

One time two of the dogs alerted at another wood rat's nest and they took it all apart but in the end nothing was found. The dogs had worked both upstream and then downstream.

As much as I appreciated all they had done and told him so, I was beyond frustrated they had not been able to go up above the mountain to the clearing that day. The land nearby was so vast, maybe over 100 acres and no search dog team would be able to comb it all, even in a few days.

Our original HRD team told me because the terrain is so thick and dense it makes it difficult for the dogs. A few inches to a few feet of leaves are compounded down on the ground. It's hard to be able to know if it's just residual scent the dogs are picking up.

I understood they exhausted all their energy while searching and worked hard to try to find some type of evidence.

I saw a lost opportunity for Darvis and I to search with the forsenic team and to speak our concerns to them.

I'm sure others spoke for us and everyone's intentions were good. However, I would have loved to have been there, even waiting on the road with no other involvement in the actual search.

When I asked McDonald what were the chances they could ever go up above where we had gone the last time, he said there would have to be more probable cause to be able to do that.

It seemed we were now at a standstill.

Looking back I knew that the Tuolumne County Sheriff's Office had done so much for us. In fact they had done pretty much all I had asked them to do.

I had been the one with the squeaky wheel, and they had done a fine job oiling it.

I realized I would have to wait for more tips to come our way.

I would have to rely on the Lord, if anything more was to be done.

I had some more investigating to do. I still had things on my list that had not been checked off yet.

Like I said before, from time to time I have had to take emotional breaks.

But then eventually I just get up and go before I can talk myself out of it.

I called Gloria and asked her if she would go out with me again. I had a couple people I wanted to talk with again. Gloria happened to be good friends with all of the people I was interested in going out to see this time.

One guy named Brad that I had wanted to see again was someone I had talked to about six months earlier. Gloria and I had went over to a house that he was staying at with Doug and Betty, the people that had lived on the same street where Mark's truck had been found and who had moved suddenly to New Mexico. I had gone there to talk with all of them. However, Doug and Betty ended up not being available, so Brad had came out and talked with me instead. He was supposed to have called me back after he talked with Doug and Betty but never had. Another couple I wanted to talk to was Paul and Kara.

Paul was the one that Darvis and I saw after Pam sent me to him, for him to tell me the *real story*. I wanted to ask them personally what they had ever heard.

The first place we were going to was in Debby's neighborhood and not far from her place.

As we drove past Debby's house even though she wasn't home, I felt a real heaviness on my heart.

I rarely came to this area anymore.

After we passed by and were heading in another direction, I suddenly had an inclination to go in the opposite direction.

I wanted to see if anyone was still living at that house where Kristie had noticed the blood spot on the deck.

When I brought up the drop of blood to Gloria, she mentioned again how a friend of hers had cut his hand on an air conditioner there as it was being carried out but I quickly said, "But what if it isn't your friend's blood?" She agreed and said, "That's true, what if it isn't?"

The last time Darvis and I had been by there, a gate had been put up and a couple of pit bulls stood guard in the driveway barking at us.

As I drove up this time, I noticed the gate was no longer there. In the driveway was so much garbage and debris that I was in shock for a moment because I had never seen such a mess before. I saw a car seat and a TV that had been thrown in one of the big piles. Children's toys and clothes of every kind were among the hundreds of items we saw. How people just walked away from all these houses and left the things they no longer wanted or could bring with them, was beyond me.

As we trampled through the garbage trying carefully to not step on anything, I noticed the old deck had been rebuilt. There was now a ramp coming off the side and plywood was put down in place of the old deck. There were no longer any steps in the front, coming up to the front door.

I noticed that the old deck from right in front of the door was still there. The old deck boards probably measured six-feet-by-four feet.

In just a moment, Gloria looked down and found what we had not been able to find the last time we had come there and said, "Isn't that a blood spot right there?"

Sure enough, right out in the open, exactly where I remember it being before, was the drop of blood.

43

I could hardly contain myself. Even though the chances of it being my son's blood were slim to none, I saw how a new door had been opened for us.

The house had been abandoned, which gave us free access to visit it again. The deck had been removed *except* for the part that I needed to see. It had been left there. The drop of blood was found *again* even when so many animals and people had trampled over it, and we hadn't even been able to find it the last time we were out there.

Now I even questioned what Cooper the detective had said about already checking out the deck and that it would be too hard to find anything after all this time anyway.

Maybe they just overlooked the exact area since we had never taken them out there and showed it to them. We had only told them about it.

Gloria and I left to go see the people I wanted to try to find.

We quickly found Brad as he did not live very far from where we were.

When I questioned him and asked him what he had found out about why Doug and Betty had moved out to New Mexico so quickly, he only told me that Doug said because he was in trouble with the law.

What seemed weird to me then, is after all that time when they finally came back into town, and he had met with Detective Bob, he was never arrested. If he had been in trouble with the law, surely he would have been arrested when he came back.

After Gloria and I left that house, we traveled to the other side of town to see if Paul and Kara were home.

When we arrived, Kara was right outside, and Gloria and her being the good friends that they were, greeted each other warmly. Gloria introduced me to Kara as Darvie's mom and she was very kind to me. She had not been home the last time Darvis and I had come by.

I was trying to wait until Paul came out to begin to ask my questions.

It took a bit of prodding for Kara to get Paul to come outside. When he did, he was gentle with his words to me, however he reminded me I had already came by before and he had told me that Pam should not be believed. I told him that I wasn't there because of Pam's story, and he kindly asked me, "Then what is it that I can help you with today?"

I asked him, "What have you personally ever heard about what happened to my son?"

He said, "Well if we had ever heard anything, we would have let Gloria know. Kara and Gloria are tight."

I brought up Louie's name because I knew he knew Louie.

I told him, "Louie has been running his mouth about my son, and I believe he knows exactly what actually happened to Darvie."

He said again that if they ever heard anything, he would let Gloria know.

Kara had no comment.

After we left, I decided not to be discouraged. The conversations with the two people I had sought out to speak with had been done.

If anything, I told Gloria, was that the word would get out and I wanted everyone to know that even over three years later, Darvie's mom was still doing her investigating.

After all, Detective Bob said I should have been a detective.

I focused my attention on the drop of blood again.

The next business day couldn't get here fast enough for me to contact McDonald. I wanted him to know what we had found.

When we finally talked on the next business day, I let him know everything.

I told him we had been given permission already from the landowner of the house to take up part of the deck if necessary.

McDonald said they would have to get written permission from the landowner if they came out.

He told me it would be best if Darvis and I could bring the piece of wood with the spot of blood on it. He told me to leave it out in the open air and not to put it in a plastic bag.

Darvis and I quickly went back up there.

Even though no one was outside, I could tell Debby was at home this time. Her vehicle was there as Darvis and I drove by. I was sickened looking at her house again. There were still the same mounds of garbage with tarps covering many things. It looked like an old junk yard.

I wondered what could be found on her property.

Darvis and I arrived at the house and I took him to the spot.

Since we had to go on the side of the house to get on the deck instead of from the front as before, it was hard to remember exactly how the deck had been in the past.

However, Darvis agreed it was exactly in the area where we had seen it before.

Darvis was going to go get his skill saw and cut it out. I started to panic when I realized that.

Knowing that Debby was home and how all the neighbors around this neighborhood were so nosy, I was too nervous for him to do that.

I was worried that the sound of the skill saw could possibly bring others over, and I did not want to see an encounter between Darvis and Debby or some of her friends.

I told Darvis that I would rather get written permission from the landlord for this exact location and have the sheriff's office come out with us.

He took a crowbar and tried to pull up the piece of deck wood. It wasn't long though and Darvis realized it was pulling up the joists and the deck piece just wouldn't budge. Darvis finally agreed with me. I would call McDonald back and ask them to come out.

I typed up a letter giving us written permission to do whatever we had to do at that exact house and I got the landlord's signature. I called and left a message with McDonald telling him what had transpired and how their assistance was now needed.

A couple of days later when I suddenly had some free time, I got the awaited call from McDonald. He wanted to know when we were able to go back out there. I told him that we were available immediately, if they were. He had to check with his crime scene investigator to see if they could go out. He said he would call me right back which he did and he said they would soon meet us at the house.

I was so jazzed. The Tuolumne County Sheriff's Office's willingness to come help us out was so greatly appreciated.

McDonald and the crime scene investigator arrived within minutes after we did.

We carefully made our way through all the garbage and ended up on the deck. I showed them what I believed to be a drop of blood.

As the crime scene investigator was preparing to get everything ready to take a tiny bit of the specimen, my mind started playing games. I started to think maybe it was just a drop of car oil and I was just wasting their time.

The crime scene investigator took a tiny swab from the drop and put it in a solution. Within seconds she looked up toward McDonald and said, "Its blood. The solution has turned blue."

44

To detect traces of blood at crime scenes, this reaction is used by criminalists. In this test, luminol powder is mixed with hydrogen peroxide and a hydroxide in a spray bottle or in a clear test tube. The luminol solution is sprayed where blood might be found or you can activate the glow either by adding potassium ferricyanide to the solution or with a drop of blood.

The iron from the hemoglobin in the blood serves as a catalyst for the chemiluminescence reaction that causes luminol to glow, so a blue glow is produced where there is blood. Only a tiny amount of iron is required to catalyze the reaction. The blue glow lasts for about 30 seconds before it fades, which is enough time to take photographs of the areas so they can be investigated more thoroughly.

After it was confirmed it was actually blood, the crime investigator took two big swabs to pick the rest of the specimen up and carefully put them away in secure non-contaminated containers.

Even though I really did not know whose blood it was, it still gave me hope.

Until we knew definitely that it wasn't our son's, I would continue to have hope.

Darvis asked me previously what I thought it would prove if it was our son's. I told him I did not know, but I told him it would at least give us something that we did not have.

We would have to rely on the Department of Justice (DOJ) at that time.

Before Darvis and I headed back home, we thanked them so much. I told McDonald I wasn't going to ask them to go check every deck in this neighborhood, but the things I had asked for were only things that were suspicious from the very beginning.

Now the blood sample would be taken to Department of Justice (DOJ) to be tested. The DOJ would also have it referenced against other samples they have received of other people's blood.

Kristie would make plans to come up in the near future to give her DNA in order for it to be compared to the sample to see if it was Darvie's.

If it ended up not being a match, then at least I would not have to spend the rest of my life wondering.

If it ended up being a match, it would at least give us something.

Things about this house that were always suspicious are:

1. It was an abandoned house.
2. Mark was up at that house a lot, and it had some of Debby's things up there.
3. It was on the road above Debby's house but not very far from it.
4. It was secluded.
5. It had big four-wheel drive recent mud tracks going up the hill behind the house just like Mark's truck would have left that we noticed originally right after Darvie had gone missing, when we were at the house checking out the place.
6. It had a burn pile in the driveway.

7. A neighbor said he had seen Mark and Darvie go up to the house, heard a shot, and Mark was the only one that had came back down.

   The neighbor again didn't confirm this when I questioned him about it later, but it is what he told Gloria.

8. I was told one time that someone heard that my son's blood was at this house.

   After the person was questioned, law enforcement felt like it was just another false story told to me, but under the weird circumstances, I wasn't so sure about that.

9. It had a drop of blood on the deck.

Darvis said it was understandable if someone had cut their hand while being at that house and walking on the deck.

I said that I know people who have cut their hands, but I never saw blood drop down on something.

Darvis said with the kind of lifestyles that some of these people around there live staying up all night, he could see someone very easily cutting their hand.

I said well then, I would think that there would be a whole bunch of blood drops in different places on the deck all the time.

Darvis thinks reasonably and also probably does things that way for some self preservation.

I think outside the box. I never quit having hope, and I try to do everything I can to find out things.

My heart yearns for the truth.

No matter what results we end up finding out when our daughter comes this week, it will be at least another stone that I made sure did not stay unturned.

I have possibly a long life on this earth awaiting me.

There will be more stones to turn over I'm sure.

I will never grow weary looking for the truth.

The Lord knows what I need and he has never disappointed me.

45

Well, I thought I would be done turning stones for awhile. Not that I wanted to stop. I never will stop as long as there is an opportunity to lead us closer to the truth.

Oh, how I pray I won't have to turn any stones over eventually because I will have been taken to the absolute truth one day on this earth. I pray that my heart will know that too.

But for the time being, I will continue my quest.

There has always been just that one missing *key* that we cannot figure out.

Darvis, Bobby, Kristie, and I went out again yesterday. We went out to that far away property that continues to call out to us.

We were looking for that *something* to set us free.

We all had somber moods as we walked the long distance down.

Leaves thickly padded our walking trails. Overgrown bushes dared us to enter.

Things were not as we remember the first time we stepped foot on this land almost four years ago.

The silence is deafening. The wildlife is scarce.

Questions were asked among us all. We were trying to figure out what happened. We were trying to look at things logically. We discussed the facts.

No one does the perfect murder.

How could someone outsmart us?

Hours later when we were leaving, new plans were made. Plans that give me new hope.

One thing though that I thought was strange are the words on the metal gate where Chuck the landowner had written, "You will bleed. You will hurt, and keep the f—— out." Some of the words were no longer there. Now it said, "I will catch you."

How strange to now have those words painted on it.

Since we were back in the vicinity again, I wanted to stop back at that area where we had previously found all those animal bones. So Kristie and I hiked down the fifty yards to try to find them again.

Previously when Darvis and I had come here, and I had gone down the embankment by myself, the grass was so overgrown. Even though I knew the bones were down there, my time was limited and with no one making the hike with me at that time, discouragement soon set in. I could not find them.

Then when the HRD team came and said they had seen no bones and that their one dog did not pick up on anything, we were at a standstill unless we made another trip out there on our own.

I already knew we would go out again eventually. It was just a matter of time.

The grass on the hillside was not so overgrown this time. The recent days of constant rain though made our heavy boots sink. It was more difficult to hike down the embankment. The manzanita trees were still so hard to climb through.

It wasn't long and we began to see the bones all over the place.

Many were obviously animal bones as we found the skulls and eye socket frontals and jaws with some teeth remaining but not all we could recognize.

My husband thinks this is a place where people dump their dead animals. I said there would be decaying animals then.

My theory is—since I know that all the animals didn't die right there and an animal is bringing the pieces here, who is to say what else could have been brought here?

Kristie carried the bones back up the mountain.

I will take them to McDonald. He already expects me.

I am so thankful that God sent us McDonald after Detective Bob retired. Another believer like us sent our way. He prays for the truth for us too I know.

McDonald has always seemed to care. At the very beginning, he came out on his own to search. He is checking into things that haven't been done yet. He is seeing things with new eyes. That is just what I prayed for.

I truly appreciate everything that Detective Bob and McDonald have done for us.

My daughter has given her DNA and it will be compared with the DNA's drop of blood we found. The results may take some time as new current prosecuting cases will take precedence.

People ask me what my mother's intuition tells me.

I believe in my heart that Mark did something to my son. I believe there were definitely others involved. Besides Mark and Louie, there is always *at least* one other name that we are always missing.

Mark was a lot smaller than Darvie's six-foot tall and 220-pound frame but Louie wasn't.

Whether they ditched him, beat him up, drugged him, or left him for dead, I do not know.

However…

I think Chuck the landowner arrived shortly after that.

The Lord has never given me clarity of his innocence.

I believe there must be a reason for that.

One time I had mentioned to Detective Bob that you would think Mark would have been blaming the landowner all along. Detective Bob surprised me by telling me that Mark *had* been blaming the landowner.

That sure made me start to wonder.

Sometimes I think two horrible things happened to my son—by two different groups of people.

I just think that Chuck the landowner made contact with someone at least once on his property even though he says he didn't. I believe he definitely knows something he hasn't told anyone.

I pray that someone who knows the 'real' truth through reading this book will have compassion and once and for all come forward.

Anyone can give tips to the Tuolumne County Sheriff's Office anonymously by calling 1-209-533-5815. If someone will come forward and take us to where our son is with the absolute truth without a shadow of doubt, we will pay them $50,000.

Detective Bob always told me that someone will eventually get mad at someone else and come forward with the truth, *or* finally get clean off of the drugs and want to do the right thing and come forward, *or* someone will get in big trouble and will want to plea bargain if they can tell what they know about our situation.

There have been several people that I have mentioned in this book that have ended up eventually getting busted and arrested and been sent to jail or prison. But still no one comes forward.

Often I've had people that I have talked with tell me that the truth will eventually come out. They have said that it *will* happen.

No matter who they are, I have held on to their words.

I've thought that maybe Louie and Mark did something to Darvie, and whether or not the landowner showed up right away, they may have left him somewhere.

Then within a few days, because Mark knew that Louie knew what had happened to Darvie, and because he didn't trust Louie completely, Mark may have tried to poison Louie at that time.

That could be why Louie was so willing to blame Mark for his poisoning even while Mark was still alive in prison.

The more Mark was questioned though, the more his story changed.

Mark didn't have a motive to do anything to Darvie, but Debby and some of her acquaintences in Oregon did. What Darvie could have exposed about some people would be unbelievable.

Darvie himself told me that he was turning in someone for the illegal things that they were doing.

I believe that this all could have started by Mark getting a phone call telling him that they wanted Darvie beat up or done away with.

Being the kind of person that I heard Mark was, that's all it took.

So my sweet son I believe was lured to Debby. Darvie always wanted to believe the best in people and wanted to be accepted by all.

Mark happened to be someone who unfortunately hung out far away out on that property.

Darvie had only gotten back in contact with them for only maybe a week.

Gloria told me that Debby told her once that if she was ever involved in a murder, she would not change the way she lived at all. She said she would live like nothing ever happened.

Seems that is exactly what she is doing.

Everyone around that neighborhood gets busted and arrested but for whatever reason, law enforcement has left Debby alone. People who are known drug dealer's should be stopped.

Debby though acting like she was a friend of Darvie's never went to his service or even offered to help us search.

Darvie didn't owe a drug debt either.

Just because my son had suffered with his drug addiction in the past doesn't mean that he *wasn't* drugged against his will that night.

I am so sad that Darvie even got in contact with Mark, a person he hardly knew.

I think he probably did get lured there because Mark had dated Darvie's estranged wife before, and maybe Darvie was trying to get with people who had known her to still feel connected.

Unfortunately that brought Debby back into his life.

I wish I would have known all these people that I have encountered who knew my son before he ever went missing.

Maybe then we could have gotten to the situation a lot sooner and things could have been different.

Ironically I was the one through a food ministry in my church quite a few years ago who offered to bring lunches to this neighborhood. I would leave the lunch bags on the mailboxes where many of these people lived. It was offered to whoever came to get them. A note was put inside to encourage them.

I have been told that at times it was the only meal some of them had for the whole day.

Even though I knew that some of the people there had been part of my son's troubles in the past, I still wanted to help them.

Now ironically, it is the same neighborhood that is still to this day being fed meals left on mailboxes by others on a weekly basis that housed the people who may have hurt my son.

One time, a couple of years ago, I felt led to drop off my own lunches again, and I put a note inside each of them. In my note, I told about my son and asked them to please call me if they knew anything.

I was hoping others would see the lunches before Debby would so she couldn't take them all away before they were able to read the note.

I never heard back from anyone.

Gloria and I tacked up new flyers with Darvie's picture on it about a year ago on a few particular streets in that neighborhood but they were soon taken down.

At least I wanted to let them know I had not forgotten, and I was still around.

No one has ever really brought us to anything tangible. Sometimes I think all the people I have talked to, never really knew what happened. Which would explain why no one has been able to take us to the truth.

I think they've all been told that Darvie cannot be found so no one looks for him.

If I didn't think my son was buried out there somewhere, I would have to let it go.

I still think he can be found.

No one has ever given me any proof otherwise.

Darvie's wallet, eye glasses and cell phone have never been found.

By hearing over and over the same horrible scenario, it made me so afraid that it would be the truth. However, I found out by reading a true story recently, where a rumor had been told over and over again. Even though the probability seemed like it must have been true, didn't make it true after all.

Darvie could have been ditched by Mark and Louie after something happened, and Chuck the landowner found Darvie lagging behind. Chuck could have had a gun and told Darvie to follow him to his vehicle.

Chuck could have gotten away with doing that.

Chuck could have taken him up to the old man Henry's property. He could be buried up there. He could be anywhere.

But where would we begin to look?

Chuck seems to be very obsessed with his property.

If Darvie and Chuck had an encounter, with Darvie losing his life, that would make more sense of why Chuck would get so mad to the point that he came back to Darvie's clothes and shot them up. No one does that without being furious.

A coworker of Chuck's had mentioned to someone that I know that Chuck had run his mouth about my son at work.

There would be no reason for Chuck to *ever* say *anything* negative about Darvie. Remember he said that he never saw him and I know that he never knew him.

How I pray a hunter or fishermen or hikers someday will come upon something *and* call law enforcement.

Just because some places are private property, doesn't mean my son went there willingly.

I still have a few things I hope will be done by law enforcement in the near future.

I want Chuck's work schedule during that time to be checked out. I want to somehow *really* know that Chuck had a *real* lie detector test. I want him questioned even more. I'd like to know why he had that cut on his forehead.

I want Chuck's ex-girlfriend, to be talked to. She has to know something.

I would like that crowbar that we found with a substance on it to be checked out more thoroughly.

I may possibly want that woman named Maria to take a lie detector test just to see if she can pass it. If she doesn't pass it, I may have to lean more toward the first scenario that we ever heard.

I would like the sheriff's office to start questioning Louie again. He has run his mouth way too long. I would like them to make Louie go out with them to the property and show them just exactly where the mine is he kept talking about.

Maybe there is another mine.

I would like Kevin questioned again by law enforcement about the argument he told me Mark and Darvie had. I just recently stopped by his house and asked him about it, but his story has changed.

I would like the sheriff's office to locate Tim again and question him further because even though I do not think he was involved, I believe that he does know something. He has since moved away to the state of Kansas.

I would like Doug and Betty questioned again. I will always believe they know something.

I think law enforcement should continue to watch Debby and catch her in a drug deal so that she can be stopped.

I would like Karen questioned again and the man who told me he had heard with his own ears from Louie what happened to Darvie, to be at least questioned.

I would like Darvie's estranged wife Paula to be questioned and some of her acquaintances up in Oregon.

I would like old man Henry questioned. I do not believe that he has ever been talked to by law enforcement.

Darvie had a credit card from his college grant that I had asked law enforcement repeatedly from the very beginning to please check to see if anyone had tried to use it. Maybe if someone had tried to use it, there would have been surveillance, and we could see who it was.

Recently McDonald told me that he had contacted the credit card company a few times, and no matter whom he talked to was told that they did not keep records that long. Unbelievable!

It was only twelve days after we found my son's remains that Darvie's estranged wife was trying to see if she could get any remaining monies out of the account. I have the paperwork.

I would like our local law enforcement to acknowledge our son's death as a homicide. I would like them to allow other outside help from other towns to come in to do more research for us even if the case has to stay open.

The things I wish would have been done is that Darvie's car would have been impounded and checked for blood and evidence. Mark's truck impounded and checked for blood and evidence. All acquaintences of Darvie's in Oregon thoroughly questioned.

It has been said, "If you want to commit murder go to Tuolumne County."

Unfortunately I think there is some kind of brotherhood here where no one wants to turn in anyone, no matter what they do.

We have been the ones who have taken law enforcement to the location. We were the ones who had the community search and found some of our son's remains.

I always wondered why our county never had another big search for us. I always felt like if it was someone else's son and the situation different, more would have been done.

I wanted to have the property burned or everything cut down so we could search better, but I knew that would never be possible. There is just way too much land. There is around sixty acres alone with Henry's and Chuck's property combined and maybe over one hundred acres above and then some. It is a forest.

However, I will never give up.

There are some things that I still want to do, and people I want to find and talk to.

When I used to hear things, if I wasn't too careful, I would get caught up in the moment, hoping that we were once again, on to something. I don't jump anymore as fast as I used to.

Andrew, the person whose name began coming up over a year ago, as people were trying to convince me that he had killed my son, suddenly died recently. Come to find out, he was in prison the whole time my son went missing.

The rumors people start...

I've had to ask myself if I knew *who* it was who actually took my son's life and possibly *what* happened, would I still have compassion.

I believe that I would because through all this I have not hated anyone.

I really would not want my worst enemy in hell because everyone is of value to the Almighty God.

I know that no one would do the things they do that are so wrong if they realized what they are doing to themselves and their future.

I know that no sin is too great that God cannot forgive.

There is nothing anyone can do to have God love them less.

The penalty for our sin is death, but the free gift of salvation through Jesus's death on the cross for all of our sins is offered to us all.

If you are someone who would like forgiveness from God so that you can make it right with him, I pray that you ask him to forgive you for all your sins and ask the Lord to come into your heart. If you sincerely do that, his Holy Spirit will come inside you supernaturally, and you will never be the same.

Come to the Lord while you still can.

If you are someone who has actually committed a crime such as one like what has happened to my son, I pray that after you make it right with the Lord, you too will come forward so that other families such as mine can have some peace of mind and never have to wonder ever again.

You will never know what this tragedy feels like unless it happens to you one day, and I pray it never does.

Sometimes I think when we get to heaven maybe none of this will matter anymore.

I know all things will be revealed one day, and we all do have a purpose on this earth. It is all a part of a bigger plan. I can't wait to see the beautiful tapestry that God has made from these ashes.

Just around the corner...

Epilogue

When I go on walks, I wear colored T-shirts that have my son's face on the front and on the back it says, "I'm walking for my son because he can't."

I have the words "Darvis Lee Jr.—Loving Son", on my back car window.

I do this in hopes that someone will stop me one day and tell me what they know.

Do I have regrets? Absolutely!

Darvie asked me, "Mom can you just give me thirty days?"

Neither one of us knew he only had seventeen.

He was a collector of Elephants. Elephants have special meaning now.

I still say his name when calling out to my other boys.

I still take double looks when I see a man walking the highways.

Just a few days before he went missing, he was down in his room. We heard him crying.

Life will never be the same.

We don't even have a headstone or a place to lay flowers in memory of him.

I will never forget the funny way that he would roll his eyes when I was trying to talk to him, and how we said 'shellfish' to each other in a way only we understood.

Answering his phone calls and hearing him saying, "Yah!" or talking serious with him and hearing him say "You wanna fight?"

I will not forget those things.

I will continue to go to his Facebook site for solace, as long as I am able to.

I always expected to receive the truth and collapse with the finality of it all. But that was not the way it was to happen.

It may seem like God has not been answering. He is just not answering the way that I expected him to.

I know you can't put God in a formula, but I expected things to have happened differently than they did. I had seen him work in such miraculous ways in no time at all before.

However, I know that I do not see the big picture. I know that he can be trusted. I know that he has it all under control. I cannot deny his hand throughout this whole ordeal that we have had to go through.

I know God has always had our best interest in mind.

What I think is ironic is that when I started this book thirteen months ago, there were six things that I had wanted done by the Tuolumne County Sheriff's Office. Throughout this whole time, God has seen that *all* six things have been done.

And that as my book is closing we are right now exactly where we are in life.

I will now have to wait.

I am waiting to turn another stone until there are no more.

I know that this has been our journey, not our son's.

We have never expected any arrests to ever be made; however, my husband has always wanted to know who is responsible for our son's death. I just want his remains found.

I know that Darvie trusted the Lord to forgive him and that he is no longer here with us, but as a mother, to think as hard of a life our son had and to be laying somewhere disrespected breaks my heart.

I know I will have to rest in the Lord until I find out one day.

Detective Bob told me from the beginning that I needed to write all this down. Even though I didn't at the time, my heart has never forgotten.

I've had to walk away from writing, or I will never stop. This story must be told.

Please pray for our family.

I must drive by Chuck the landowner's house every day to get to my home.

I can't stop at my own mailbox without a thought coming my way of a man who did such a mean thing to my son's belongings.

Someday I hope to move away...

I would love to be in a town where no one there knew my son, and I would never have to wonder if they knew something.

I would love to not have to see so many reminders.

Darvie used to tell people that he was going to be famous one day.

Well, through this book, his life though short-lived here on earth, will continue to help others.

Part of the proceeds of every book sold will always go to help someone.

Whether we will be able to start a foundation in his name to help other families of missing children in their search for their loved one or be able to give a scholarship at the local high school that Darvie attended, to help others going to a junior college possibly studying criminal law or forsenic science, someone will be helped.

An old Indian man has given me his blessing...

Darvie used to say when someone did something so wrong, "Unbelievable!"

I know that throughout this whole journey that is what he would have been saying. "Mom, this has been so unbelievable!"

I had a dream awhile back, and I am not one who holds on to dreams much. But I dreamed that Darvie called me on the phone. I was very excited that it was him and I told him how much I missed him. I handed the phone to his dad to have him see for himself that it was indeed really Darvie.

Darvie thought that it was still 2010 but I told him it was already 2013.

Without telling him anything, I asked him if he would like me to write a book about him. He said, "Yes."

For those of you who knew him, you already knew that answer.

He always liked being the center of attention.

When Darvie was here for those seventeen days, he talked about getting a tattoo. He even told his best friend Kathy that he wanted to make sure the tattoo was something that I would approve of.

Darvie was a kind man and wouldn't have intentionally hurt anyone.

Darvie was my biggest fan, and I know that he still is.

He's probably been rooting for me this whole time.

Remember, *'All it takes for evil to flourish is for good people to do nothing.'*

What do you think? I pray that someone reading this will know the truth and come forward once and for all.

Perhaps it's you?

Poems from My Heart

This is a collection of thirteen poems that I wrote to my son beginning from the time he went missing until over three years later. God has given me this gift, and whenever my heart prompted me, it only took pen and paper for me to release the words.

I Do Not Want

Written within one month after Darvie went missing. I started realizing what life would be like if he didn't come back. I wanted him found so badly.

I still thought we had some time.

I do not want to see my life, son, with you no longer in it,
To never hear from you again, I would not like that one bit.
I do not want to miss out on you, having children of your own,
You wanted to be a dad,
More than any man I have ever known.

I do not want to never laugh again with you,
So hard I cannot stop,
The fun times we have had together, in your eyes,
I know I was close to the top.

I do not want to not see you finish school,
And get the great job that you wanted.
You've accomplished so much, in so little time,
You really did it.

I do not want to grow old, without you with me,
You were the one who would have taken care of me,
It was the way you said it would be.

I do not want to imagine, that you are somewhere,
Out there hurt,
I know people are working hard,
We will not stop our search.

Hold on son, if you can,
I know your life has been so hard,
We believe you can make it.
In our hearts, you are not far.
So here's to not giving up on you, son.
You truly are one of the best things that ever happened to me,
I do not want to lose you now.
I pray it is not to be.

We're Coming

This poem was written when so much time had passed. By that, I just knew something must have happened to Darvie. A main person of interest was now being questioned regarding his disappearance. We still couldn't find Darvie, and I wanted him to know we were not giving up.

If you're missing us and don't know what to do.
If you think this is a nightmare, like we do too.
Don't worry, son, "We're Coming".

If there're
many things you can't wait to tell us.
That you feel you'll go crazy if you have to wait...
But must.
Don't worry son, "We're Coming".

If you have regrets...
From when you were down here with us.
Just know...that everyone does.
Don't worry, son, "We're Coming".

If it seems to you, like we have the wrong "man".
If it looks like we haven't done all that we can.
Don't worry, son, "We're Coming".

If it looks to you like you'll never be found.
That it seems to you
That we haven't covered much "ground".
Don't worry, son. "We're Coming"

If you ever wondered how much you were loved.
I know now you are being shown how much,
From God up above.
Don't worry, son, "We're Coming".

If you can't bear the thought of not seeing us for years.
Just know when we get there, even the angels will cheer.
Don't worry, son, "We're Coming".

We're coming, son, please have no doubt.
You can be sure that their sins will find them out.
Our Heavenly Father has heard our prayers.
He will not allow more than we can bear.
He has never failed us or let us down.
We put our complete trust in him. Soon you will be found.

While We Wait

Written as I began to see the hand of God while we were trying to find the answers. I saw horrible things, and yet beautiful things as this nightmare of events began to happen as we were trying to find Darvie.

While we wait...
Our minds have filled with unanswered questions.
Our hearts have been broken in two, so many times
We have questioned how man
Is capable of doing such horrible things.
We have seen people who may have the answers,
But choose not to care.
We have traveled to places
We would never have journeyed before.
We see how the enemy
Has truly messed up so many people's lives.

But...
As we wait...
We see our questions being answered.
Though our hearts still hurt,
We trust in the One who sees all our tears.
We see how man
Also is capable of doing such wonderful things.
We see people who do care
And who take the chances by doing the right thing.
We have found some of the nicest people
In places where our paths may never of crossed.
We see good overcoming evil,
In the lives where the enemy no longer has any power.

Through it all, we have clung to our Lord who has been our shelter through this storm. The *one* whose right hand has upheld us, who has heard our cry, came down from heaven, sent his messengers to fulfill his wishes, rescued us from our enemies, showed us the way that we should go, been our rock, our stronghold and our deliverer. Our shield is in whom we take refuge, who subdue people under us. He has been gracious and compassionate. Rich in love. Faithful to his promises. He has been near. His favor has been upon us. He has not treated us as our sins deserve or repaid us according to our iniquities.

> For as high as the heavens
> Are above the earth,
> So great is his love for those who fear him.
> We will remember the wonder he has done,
> His miracles,
> And the judgments
> He pronounced throughout all of this.
> His greatness no one can fathom.
> We know one day, the truth will set us free.

No Time For Good-byes

This was written when I began to realize all that we missed out on with how abruptly things transpired. I felt like we were left with no time for anything that mattered.

No "time for good-byes" is what my heart would say,
No "one last hug" to try to hold us over,
Until the long awaited day.

No "last words" prepared to say to you,
No "one last glance" knowing how important,
It would have been to do.

You left way too soon for our hearts to understand,
And we had no idea what we ourselves
Were about to withstand.

The sleepless nights, the tears to shed,
The constant dreams and nightmares,
That we have come to dread.

A new sadness we have never felt,
And a knowledge that has been hard to bear.
To see how, at the core of man,
The evil that some have even dared.

The desperation of needing to find you,
And the frustration of letting go.
Is something that has went on way too long,
God, PLEASE, PLEASE, let us know.

No "time for good-byes" is what my heart would say,
No place to lay some flowers,
To show others you went away.

And though my heart is broken,
Filled with regret of things we never got to do.
I know that "your love" will always carry me through.

Your love" will remind me,
That you are saying, "I'll see you soon, Mom".
It will remind me of your loving hugs,
That won't be gone for long.

It will remind me of your words,
Spoken kindly about me.
And it will remind me of "You",
And that soon "You" again I will see.

My Biggest Fan

This poem was what I wrote for the service of Darvie's Celebration of life that my daughter Kristie read. I began to realize just how much Darvie loved me.

My biggest fan has gone away,
To a place I do not know of yet.
Where there is no more sadness, no more pain,
Only love, the best that you can get.

To think that many years may pass me by,
Before we meet again.
Gives me a sadness I have never felt,
A pain that will always win.

What will I do without you by my side?
To cheer me on in life?
Through the good and the bad?
And the times where we can only cry?

The loyalty that you always showed me,
I know was God's plan from above.
You honored me as your Mom, for which I am very grateful,
And your love… your wonderful love.

To think my world didn't stop,
When my heart broke in two.
Sadly life must go on,
Going forward is something I have to do.

Now I will grow old without you,
Something that wasn't supposed to be.
Someone, somewhere, got it all wrong,
Or at least that's what it seems like to me.

But I know God is good,
And he has it all figured out.
And someday when we see the big picture,
It will remove all our doubt.

Because it's true they say, you had to go before me.
To fix up my mansion, just so.
I know you will be waiting and watching for me,
To take me to meet our Heavenly Father, is where we will go.

So don't worry about me son,
Someday we will be together again.
To worship for an eternity,
The Lord Jesus who took away our sin.

Six Months Today

Written six months after Darvie went missing. It was so hard to believe that all that time had already went by.

Six months today,
Oh tell me it isn't so.
We did not know you were going away,
I wish you didn't have to go.

Thirty six years we had you,
Your love we always felt.
All the things we wished we would have done,
Has left us feeling so much guilt.

We didn't see this coming,
Why would someone want to hurt you?
You were so kindhearted,
Helping others is what you would always do.

You always saw the good in people,
Being needed by others is what you loved.
You never refused to lend a helping hand,
Worth it or not, it was the way it always was.

No one loved you more,
Than your family that was always close by,
But you spent your life wanting to be accepted,
By others, we never knew why.

No one can take away the memories
We shared with you,
No one can take away the love that will never die.
For a season, we may be kept apart,
Even though we do not know why.

But the laughter we will have again,
Oh I look forward to that day.
We will embrace and never want to let go,
But we will know it is a future that will never go away.

You will be watching for us I know.
To see who will be next to go.
Helping to welcome us into our glorious home,
To a life we have never known.

We have our faith,
The only way we know how to cope.
Is by resting in the Almighty's arms,
He has given us this hope.

He gives us peace beyond all understanding,
In a time where turmoil is all around.
He picks us up through the raging storms,
And has placed us on higher ground.

Someday we will see the big picture,
And marvel at all his awesome ways.
And be so grateful that you too trusted him,
As we begin our never-ending days.

I Can't Put Into Words

I couldn't believe time just kept going on. Eight months! Tips were slowing down. Stories were changing. I felt so frustrated but continued to trust the Lord.

I can't put into words, what I'm feeling right now,
Almost eight months has passed by, all I can say is "WOW!"

Time has marched on, not waiting for us to catch up,
And yet things have slowed down,
Which has made it real tough.

Things that could have been done, to help us in our case,
Have seemed to be at a standstill,
Making it all seem like such a waste.

People knowing the truth and not telling, and others hiding out,
In my own hometown,
Makes me wonder about the humanity of man,
And leaves me with a lot of doubt.

I know the truth will one day be revealed,
The ones responsible will be taken down,
But to sit and wait for justice to be done,
Makes me want to move out of this town.

My loved one is missing, someone I care about so much,
People chose to make bad decisions,
Not realizing the lives that it would touch.

Someone needs to do the right thing,
And get it off their chest,
To confess it here, before they meet their Maker,
Really would be best.

Though I get frustrated and learning patience is so very hard,
I trust in the *one* who sees my pain,
Who's been with me from the very start.

He will make *beauty* from these *ashes*,
He will comfort me in my mourning,
He will make all things new one day
And I will give him all the glory.

Wasn't Ready For Good-bye

Ten months, and I still wasn't ready to say good-bye.

I wasn't ready for good-bye, when you went away.
Nothing seemed any different, same as any other day.
But it didn't take long to see, something wasn't right.
From a mom's intuition I knew,
You wouldn't have chosen to vanish out of sight.

You and I were too connected,
We had a love that made sure of that.
We wouldn't have went many days,
To not know where each other was at.

In ten months, we have encountered people,
That had never crossed our path.
You would have wanted to protect us from them,
But yet proud how we've filled in the gap.

We have searched and searched, and still search today.
Dad and I and your sister won't stop,
Until we get our way.

We get so close it seems,
And then we get stopped again.
Yet even through all that, the truth is coming in.

We are waiting for that one person,
Who can really help us out.
As we wait on our Heavenly Father,
Who is doing unseen wonders for us, no doubt.

We know we will be with you, again one day.
The waiting is the hardest,
But with patience we will find a way.

I wasn't ready for Good-bye,
I didn't want you to go away.
My heart will always feel a little empty,
Until that long awaited day.

One Year Ago

One year! How life continued to go on was beyond me.

One year ago our world was shattered,
Finding you safe was all that mattered.

When we realized on this earth that was not to be so,
The searches began to wherever we needed to go.

We've worked so hard, following every lead,
Even gone to dangerous places trying to satisfy our need.

We've heard from so many who have really known nothing
   at all.
But a whole bunch of hearsay from those who supposedly
   'heard' and who supposedly 'saw'.

Who just wanted to be a 'part'
But their words have torn us in two, actually broke our hearts.

And we've heard from others who really have cared,
Who have tried to lighten our burden and make our sorrow
   not so hard to bear.

We will not stop until we get the answers we need,
Eventually we will find the missing key.

One long year of sadness and pain,
I know our lives will never be the same.

But our Lord has been with us through it all,
He has seen every single one of our teardrops fall.

He has all the answers, so we cling to him,
We know in the end evil will be conquered and good will win.

You really are safe now no one can hurt you anymore.
The trust and faith we claim to have cannot be ignored.

Because that is what will help us survive,
Through all the years here that we will be alive.

Before we ever see you again, we too have a story that has a
beginning and an end.
And I want to live it, to bring glory to Him.
And we will have an eternity together, better than it has
ever been.

Happy Birthday Son

Written on Darvie's second birthday without him.
Twenty-one months had already gone by.

Happy Birthday, Son,
Thirty-eight, you are today.
Another one without you,
We'd come see you, if there was a way.

Sending a balloon up in the sky,
Baking you a cake.
Then Brother, Dad and I,
Are taking a drive to a lake.

This has been a real hard road for us,
Living without you.
We never signed up for this,
But there is nothing we can do.

Life took a different turn,
You suddenly went away.
And Son for twenty-one months, we've missed you so,
Dealt with everything that's come our way.

So wherever you are today,
Whatever plans you have made.
Know that we are here honoring you.
On your very special day.

I See the People

This was written when I began to realize how much Darvie might yearn for the day that I will join him in heaven. We had a connection that couldn't be denied.

Although I didn't believe that being around the Lord would make anyone yearn for anyone else, I wrote it as if he just missed me and couldn't wait to see me.

I see the people, all coming in,
To join their loved ones, a wonderful life to begin.
It makes me happy, to see it all being done,
But Lord please tell me, when is my Mom?

I know people who aren't here yet,
Have purposes to fulfill,
I know she would want to finish that,
And to do your will.
And I know she is needed there, don't get me wrong,
But Lord please help me, I'm missing my Mom.

I know she is happy taking care of all she does,
There wasn't a child she couldn't love, never was.
But I know her so well. Her heart has hurt till it's raw,
So Lord please tell me, when I get to be with my Ma?

We had such a connection. We were so much alike,
Laughing and talking, and starting our fights.
I know you gave us loved ones,
To teach us what's to come,
But Lord I keep wondering, where is my Mum?

I can't wait to see her. We will have so much to say,
I look so forward to it,
And I know she can't wait for that day.
I try to be patient. I try to stay calm,
I try to keep busy, waiting for my Mom.

So until that day Lord, will you keep her safe?,
Help her to stay happy, keep her strong in the faith.
Help her to know, one day she will be in awe,
When she sees her Son, and I see my Ma.

Saying Good-bye

This was written after Darvie had been gone for over three years. I was finally ready to let his travel trailer go. I would walk by it at night and cry. I would go inside of it and just be in such unbelief that the person that was so alive in it, just a few years earlier, was no longer coming back.

You'd think I'd already said it,
After all this long, long, time.
But my heart just wasn't ready,
Searching for something I couldn't find.

I didn't want to believe,
That you were really gone for good.
I've held on for so long,
As tightly as I could.

You should be here!
You shouldn't be away!
This mama still wanted you!
I expected you to stay!

But no matter what I hold onto,
It will never bring you back.
I can sit and cry about it,
But you're gone and that's a fact.

No matter how much I miss your calls,
Your daily check-in times.
It's been nearly three years now,
Since someone cut our lines.

So I will try to let a little go,
It won't be a whole bunch.
But I will say good-bye to things,
That holding on to hurts too much.

Because I don't need reminders,
Of the loss my heart has felt.
Sometimes looking at things,
May just produce more guilt.

Cobwebs, dust, and emptiness,
Is all that fills some things.
The moments in time that were once there,
Sadness now is all it brings.

I will say good-bye to some of those,
It may destroy if I let it remain.
I will say good-bye and look away,
And know the peace that I will gain.

This life is but a speck,
In all of eternity.
It really won't be long,
Until my son I will see.

Because he too trusted Jesus,
To make him whole again.
To be cleansed from all unrighteousness,
Delivered from this life of sin.

So that my heart will start to heal,
I will not hold on so tightly anymore.
Because I know what's best for me,
Is right beyond this open door.

No Unturned Stone

Written when I was almost done writing this book.
I was explaining what I meant by "No Unturned Stone."

No unturned stone,
The way it has to be.
I won't stop until I know for sure,
The truth may set me free.

A long journey this has been,
Turning stone after stone.
No matter how heavy it has been,
The Lord has not left me alone.

He has opened doors with just the right key,
He has amazed me with every step.
This journey has surely been a lesson to learn,
My teardrops he has kept.

He has seen every one,
He has held me, oh so close.
I couldn't have made it without him by my side,
In him, I want to boast.

Every tip I have checked out,
Every person I have sought.
Who may possibly know the answer,
The fight with good and evil I have fought.

So until The Lord removes the stones,
And his hand I do not see.
There will be no unturned stone,
The way it has to be.

Truly a gift from God.

Fun Loving Little Man.

The beginning of our bonding.

The start of our family.

Feeling so loved.

When life was still so innocent.

My pride-n-joys!

Right before the damage was done and our son was kidnapped.

Good times with his Aunt Carolyn not long before she passed away.

Always dressed in style.

Celebrating life!

What a smile!

Darvie and his Dad.

Trying to make changes.

Trying to make more changes.

Better Days!

Right after the rescue from the mine. We were
so grateful to have our son back.

Good memories. Darvie, Bobby, and Kristie.

A rare picture of us all together. Darvie, Kristie, Darvis and I.

He always liked having our picture taken together.

Darvie and his younger sister Kerri.

My son and I, only four months before he lost his life.

His eyes seem to tell a story.

Darvie's Facebook Profile Picture.

Never knew how much this picture would mean to us.

One of the flyers that I had made.

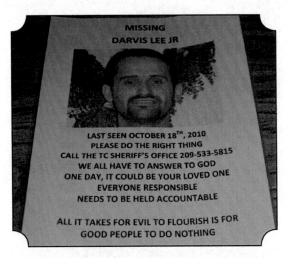

Another flyer that I had made and taped on to my car windows.

"When the butterflies come, you can think of your son."
The Monarch butterfly that landed!

Our beautiful Hydrangea plant that keeps on growing.

First bud on the eve of his birthday.

The first Rose of Sharon flower opened up in full bloom.

The flowers that appeared while I was writing the chapter about them.

Releasing our first balloon, one year after he went missing.

The constant brush that we have had to trample
through on our many searches.

"Catch ya later"